A treasure hunter's guide

bottles, relics and gems

A treasure hunter's guide

bottles, relics and gems

by

Edward Fletcher

Blandford Press

First published 1975
by Blandford Press Ltd,
Link House, West Street, Poole, Dorset BH15 1LL
© Edward Fletcher 1975

ISBN 0 7137 0741 0

Text set in 12 on 13 Bembo and
printed in Great Britain by
Unwin Brothers Ltd
The Gresham Press
Old Woking, Surrey

Contents

Acknowledgements

The author and publishers wish to thank the following for providing some of the photographs in this book:

Borough of Falmouth: Figs. 19, 20
Western Mail and Echo: Fig. 22
S. Kruk-Schuster, Poulton-le-Fylde: Fig. 29
Inland Waterways Association: Fig. 35
John Quigley: Figs. 46, 49
Northumbria Tourist Board: Fig. 53
East Midlands Tourist Board: Fig. 57
Scottish Tourist Board: Figs. 73, 74, 75, 76, 77, 78
Michael Allman: Fig. 79 and cover photograph

Author's Note

The county boundaries mentioned in this book and used on the maps are those which were in force before 1 April 1974.

Introduction

Since publication of the four earlier titles in this series (*Pebble Polishing; Rock and Gem Polishing; Bottle Collecting; Treasure Hunting For All*) the hobbies with which they are concerned have come to the attention of most people in Britain. Those who have not yet read the books have seen on their television screens or in newspaper and magazine illustrations the fascinating Victorian relics recovered by bottle collectors, the valuable coins unearthed by amateur treasure hunters, and the colourful semi-precious gemstones found and transformed to beautiful jewellery by Britain's rockhounds. These hobbies are no longer the pursuits of an eccentric minority; they are national pastimes enjoyed by a substantial percentage of those who seek creative leisure activities providing equally stimulating exercise for body and mind.

Publicity alone will not sustain the growth of hobbies that do not satisfy those who take them up. To conclude that bottle collecting, rockhounding, and amateur treasure hunting have achieved their present popularity simply because books have been written about them and newspaper editors and television producers have found them worthy of copy and viewing time is to put the horse at the wrong end of the cart. It is the finds made by bottle diggers, coin-shooters and rockhounds that have attracted widespread publicity; but it is because many of these finds were made by newcomers with limited experience and equipped with only simple and inexpensive tools that others have decided to join in and have found, to their great satisfaction, they can match these successes by following a few straightforward rules. Thus has a busy housewife in Buckinghamshire dug up one of the most valuable collections of monochrome pot lids in Britain; thus has a London schoolboy recovered from the foreshores of the Thames a harvest of coins dating from pre-Roman times to the present century; thus has a Yorkshire rockhound found jet, freshwater pearls, fluorite, amethyst, and other gemstones from which he has made unique and beautiful jewellery. All over Britain thousands of men, women and children have proved to themselves that success at these hobbies is not limited to a fortunate few. It can be found, as can bottles, pot lids, pipes, coins, jewellery, badges and semi-precious gems, by all who seek.

The earlier books in this series are mainly concerned with the basic techniques of each hobby. *Pebble Polishing* explains how to achieve perfect results with a simple tumbler; *Rock and Gem Polishing* covers the use of more advanced lapidary machines; in *Bottle Collecting* I have explained the techniques of site research, digging, and find cleaning, while *Treasure Hunting for All* covers the correct methods of using detectors and other coin and relic hunting tools. In this present book I offer a guide to many of the best rockhounding sites, bottle dumps, and amateur treasure hunting locations in the country. It has been written to meet the needs of those enthusiasts who wish to pursue the hobbies in unfamiliar regions of Britain, either during their holidays or on week-end trips to areas about which they have no local knowledge. It is not offered as a substitute for the detailed research every reader should undertake concerning sites close to home. Experienced rockhounds, dump diggers, and amateur treasure hunters who live in any of the counties included in the guide will certainly have considerable local knowledge of many sites not suggested here. The usefulness of this guide to such readers will, I hope, become apparent when they make holiday journeys of many miles and do not wish to spend valuable time in public libraries and city archives trying to locate sites on which to enjoy their precious holiday hours.

Although much of the information in the guide has come from personal records and notes made during years of interest in all three hobbies, I am indebted to members of the British Bottle Collectors Club, the British Amateur Treasure Hunting Club, and to many of my rockhounding acquaintances for additional information on sites in those areas to which my travels have not yet taken me and about which I know very little. I am also grateful for advice and suggestions from my friends on where new and undis- covered sites might lie in any of the counties covered in the guide. I hope readers will use the clues provided to locate and open up these sites for the benefit of all because new sites are the lifeblood of our hobbies.

Newcomers to rock-hounding, coinshooting, and bottle collecting who have not yet read the earlier books may be unaware of the importance of obtaining landowner's permission *before* a search or a dig is carried out on any site. To those readers I say: You have no inalienable right to dig anywhere other than in your own back garden; if you do so without permission on any other site you could find yourself in conflict with the law, and you will certainly breach the rules on this subject by which all members of The British Bottle Collectors Club and The British Amateur Treasure Hunting Club abide. In practice it is rarely difficult to obtain the necessary permission no matter which of the three hobbies you hope to pursue. Rockhounds will find that many of the mines, quarries, and gravel pits they visit are at work seven days a week and that there is usually a manager or foreman on the site to whom polite requests for permission to search spoil heaps can be addressed. Such permission will almost certainly be granted on condition that site work is not interrupted and that searches for rock and crystal specimens are not carried out in danger areas. The rockhound who wishes to collect pebbles on seaside beaches is not required to obtain permission from the local corporation if he limits to a bucketful the pebbles removed; but it should be noted that there are several privately owned beaches and islands around our coasts from which it is forbidden to remove material including rocks and pebbles. Prominently displayed signboards should indicate the locations of such sites.

Many of Britain's nineteenth-century rubbish dumps are located on derelict land around river estuaries and alongside disused canals. In spite of their desolate and abandoned appearance they are owned by landlords whose permission must be obtained before digging commences. The British Bottle Collectors Club has already obtained permission for club digs on many of these sites; if you become a member you will be able to take part in these weekend activities

3

which are organized by the club's county secretaries.

If you wish to recover bottles from a refuse dump on which club digs are not organized you must write to the landowner beforehand. A polite letter which explains your interest in nineteenth-century bottle history and which assures the owner the site will be left neat and tidy at the end of your dig usually results in permission being granted. Some site owners, particularly local corporations, insist that diggers obtain insurance cover indemnifying the owner in the event of accident or injury on the site before they will grant permission. Such cover can be obtained for a few pounds from most insurance companies.

I am confident that several coin hoards will be found by readers of this book within a year of publication. The clues to the whereabouts of hidden hoards given in the following chapters are the most comprehensive yet published and there can be no doubt that some of these hoards will be located by detector owners. *You* could be one of those on whom good fortune smiles, and for that reason I warn you never to undertake a detector search on a site which might hold hidden wealth without the consent of the landowner. The best method of safeguarding your interests as a treasure hunter is to sign a written agreement with the landowner before you begin your search that all finds or Treasure Trove rewards will be shared equally with him. Further information on Treasure Trove law is given in *Treasure Hunting For All*.

There is another important reason why coinshooters should always obtain the consent of the landowner before searching a site. Many professional archaeologists hope to see a ban on detector ownership by anyone other than a professional archaeologist. This desire to prevent the general public enjoying a harmless and rewarding hobby stems from the fact that professional archaeologists have in recent years become alarmed by the number of amateur archaeologists who have stolen artifacts from sites on which they have worked under professional supervision. Unwilling to admit that this looting is carried out by amateur archaeologists, the professionals have made strenuous efforts to place

4

the blame for it solely on the heads of those members of the general public who own metal detectors.

Coinshooters suffer the brunt of this smear campaign, which is as illogical as it is vicious. None of those who make the accusations have a sound knowledge of the hobby; they fail to make a distinction between the *discarded* and usually damaged artifacts recovered on archaeological sites and the *lost* or *hidden* objects found by amateur treasure hunters on sites including footpaths, commons, riversides, beaches, gardens, houses and ploughed fields. Fortunately you do not need the approval of an archaeologist before you search a site with your detector. If you have the landowner's permission and if you abide by the amateur treasure hunters' Code of Conduct, which was drawn up with the help of the Ancient Monuments Secretariat several years ago, and which is reproduced at the end of this book, you are free to enjoy the hobby on that site regardless of the rantings of any professional archaeologist.

I hope all readers—coinshooters, bottle collectors, and rockhounds—will make exciting finds on the sites suggested in the following chapters. Those who can spare the time to write a short letter giving details of their finds or comments on the sites will earn my gratitude and help keep up-to-date records of finds compiled by The British Bottle Collectors Club and The British Amateur Treasure Hunting Club. Letters should be marked for my attention and sent to one of the clubs whose addresses are given at the end of the book. Visitors to Britain who arrive without tools and equipment and who wish to try their luck on some of the sites I have named will be able to hire or buy all necessary equipment from the suppliers listed in the addresses section. Many of these suppliers also sell bottles, rock specimens, coins and other relics; most are interested in buying from overseas markets.

Good hunting to all!

1 South-East England

The tidal foreshores of the Thames between Teddington Lock and Greenwich provide some of Britain's most productive amateur treasure hunting sites. Mud and shingle patches exposed by falling tides on both sides of the river are littered with coins, tokens, badges, jewellery, weapons and other relics of a long and exciting history from pre-Roman times to the present day; no amateur treasure hunter worthy of the name should miss an opportunity to spend time seeking them when in London. The tidal reaches are administered by the Port of London Authority, while the river above Teddington is controlled by the Thames Conservancy Board. Permission to search the river banks for amateur treasures should be sought from these bodies.

Although access to the Middlesex foreshore between Teddington Lock and Eel Pie Island is difficult without a boat, the effort to reach it can be worthwhile because many seventeenth- and eighteenth-century coin finds are made here at exceptionally low tides. From time to time the locks at Teddington and Richmond are closed simultaneously and the flow of water on this stretch reduced to a trickle. When this happens one can wade almost to the middle of the river and many fascinating finds including antique weapons and bottles can be made.

A couple of miles downstream the foreshore flanking Syon Park is a well-known and much used detector site. Coins that turn up here can be from any period, though Roman finds are the most common. There was a riverside settlement here even before Julius Caesar came to Britain, and the ford that served it continued in use until the building of the first Kew Bridge in 1789. The river here remains undredged, apart from the central channel, and the foreshore is rich in metal objects. Celtic coins, Roman coins by the hundred, ancient brooches and other jewellery, bronze axeheads, spears, medieval tokens, and a large number of silver coins from the Civil War period are all reported as finds by the hundreds of amateur treasure hunters who visit the site every year.

7

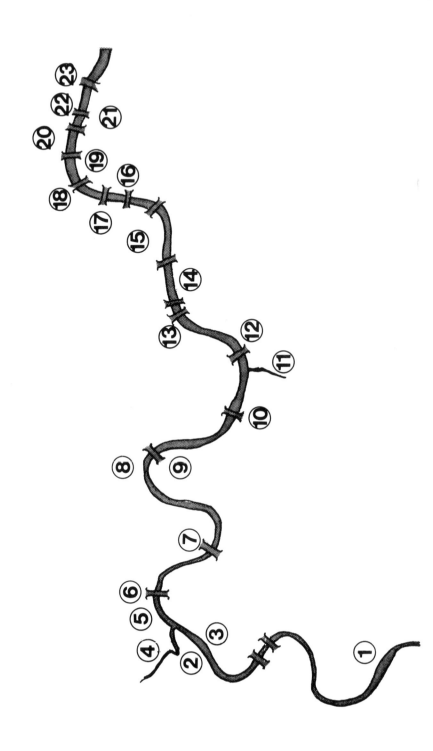

Fig. I (*left*)   The Thames: foreshore sites from Teddington Lock to Tower Bridge.

Key

1 Teddington Lock—Eel Pie Island foreshore has 17th- and 18th-century coins on Middlesex side.
2 Syon Park foreshore is rich in Celtic, Roman, medieval, and Civil War coins and relics.
3 Victorian coins on this foreshore.
4 River Brent.
5 Celtic coins on Brentford Ait.
6 18th-century coins and jewellery at Strand-on-the-Green, downstream from Kew Bridge.
7 Chiswick Bridge.
8 Coins and jewellery of all periods beneath Hammersmith Bridge.
9 Roman coins on this foreshore.
10 Putney Bridge. Many clay tobacco pipes and some bottles and coins on north foreshore upstream from bridge.
11 River Wandle.
12 Wandsworth Bridge. Celtic and Roman coins at very low tides between the bridge and the mouth of the River Wandle.
13 Battersea Bridge. Roman and Celtic relics on southern foreshore between Battersea and Wandsworth Bridges.
14 The foreshores between Albert and Chelsea Bridges near Battersea Park have many early coins and tobacco pipes.
15 Vauxhall Bridge. The southern foreshore, downstream from the bridge, has Victorian coins.
16 Lambeth Bridge.
17 Westminster Bridge.
18 Waterloo Bridge.
19 Coins of all periods can be found on foreshores near Royal Festival Hall. Bottles and pipes can be found between Waterloo and Blackfriars Bridges. Many coins and relics are to be found upstream from Blackfriars Bridge.
20 The Queenhithe foreshore, upstream from Southwark Bridge, is rich in coins and relics from the medieval to Victorian periods.
21 Many coins and relics of all periods can be found between Southwark and Tower Bridges. The foreshores near London Bridge are rich in Roman coins on very low tides.
22 London Bridge.
23 Tower Bridge.

Less attention is paid to the foreshore on the Surrey side hereabouts because much of it is buried beneath the ugly riverwall which extends for part of the distance between Richmond Footbridge and Kew Bridge. Where the wall gives way to natural vegetation large bushes and trees grow down to the water's edge. The sandy mud around their roots holds many nineteenth-century coins. There is also an unconfirmed story in London amateur treasure hunting circles of a hoard of Victorian gold spectacle frames found here some years ago.

The present Kew Bridge was opened in 1905. During its construction an arsenal of Bronze Age and Iron Age weapons were found in the river. Many more must lie in the mud below the low tide line, but so far none have been discovered on the popular detector site at Strand-on-the-Green, a few yards downstream from the bridge on the Middlesex side.

9

Fig. 2 Finds from the foreshores of the Thames.

Eighteenth-century coins and jewellery are found here by detector users who search the area just below the high tide line, while those who enjoy working with a rake and sieve can find earlier coinage lower down the foreshore.

The canalized River Brent joins the Thames half a mile above Kew Bridge and there are three islands in the main river between this point and the bridge. A hoard of pre-Roman coins was found on one of the islands in the nineteenth-century. It was probably hidden by an inhabitant of the ancient settlement near Syon Park during an attack on the ford more than two thousand years ago. Other coins have turned up on the islands in recent years and it is likely that at least one more hoard awaits discovery.

There is little amateur treasure hunting activity on the river between Chiswick and Barnes, but the foreshores on both sides of the river at Hammersmith are very popular sites where coins of all periods can be found. A Celtic coin hoard was found on the south shore at Hammersmith many years ago and a considerable number of isolated Roman

10

coins have been located by detector users in this area. It is possible that some of these coins were deposited in the nineteenth century when large quantities of gravel dredged from London Bridge were used to build up the tow paths between Hammersmith and Barnes. The river banks beneath Hammersmith Bridge, which was opened in 1827, produce Victorian coins and jewellery.

Putney Bridge is a classic site for clay tobacco pipe collectors; pipe bowls from the seventeenth to late eighteenth century can be picked up at low tide on the Middlesex foreshore a hundred yards downstream from the bridge. The spot was used in Victoria's reign as a loading area for barges carrying household refuse upriver to dumping grounds along the Grand Junction Canal and the foreshore is littered with glass and pottery fragments. Complete bottles, including Codd's and Hamilton's, can be found on very low tides. Raking and sieving also produces Victorian and modern coins.

A mile downstream from Putney Bridge, Wandsworth Creek and the River Wandle enter the Thames on the Surrey side. This area has produced some of the finest ancient weapons yet found on the riverside. A hoard of bronze axeheads was discovered near Wandsworth Gasworks many years ago; several swords and shields have turned up; and a dagger in an ornate bronze sheath was picked up by a mudlark working the area between Wandsworth Bridge and the mouth of the Wandle. More recently, Celtic and Roman coins have been found by amateur treasure hunters raking and sieving the exposed bed at low tide.

It was from the riverbed between Wandsworth Bridge and Battersea Bridge that the most spectacular Iron Age treasure yet found in the river—the Battersea Shield—was dredged in the nineteenth century. This is now in the British Museum, as are many other Celtic and Roman finds from this part of the Thames. The southern foreshore upstream from Battersea Bridge also holds many relics of London's later history; coins of the fifteenth and sixteenth centuries have been found here by detector users. The foreshore flanking Battersea Park is another site much frequented by London's amateur treasure hunting fraternity. A catalogue of finds by one enthusiast during a single year gives some idea of the finds to be expected by those who visit this site: decorated pipe bowls, Elizabethan silver coins, Charles I farthings, eighteenth-century lead and copper tokens, Victorian jewellery, nineteenth-century gold, silver and copper coins, and several early twentieth-century medals.

The narrow stretch of undredged foreshore on the southern side of the river downstream from Vauxhall Bridge does not produce so varied an assortment of finds, but it is rich in nineteenth-century coins. Recently large numbers of Victorian one-third farthings have been found here by amateur treasure hunters who have passed mud and gravel through fine mesh sieves. From this point to Hungerford Bridge the Thames is imprisoned by embankments on both sides of the river with very little foreshore exposed by the falling tides because the banks have been deeply dredged. At Hungerford a patch of undredged foreshore near the Royal Festival Hall can be profitably searched using the rake and sieve method. Most of the finds are Victorian, though seventeenth- and eighteenth-century relics occasionally turn up. It is possible to walk along the southern riverside at low tide from this site to Blackfriars Bridge and finds can be made almost anywhere along the route. There are many glass and stoneware bottles because this area, like the Putney Bridge site already mentioned, was used by Victorian London's refuse barges. Household rubbish loaded onto barges here was taken to dumping grounds on the Essex and Kent marshes.

There was a medieval dock on the southern riverside a few yards upstream from Blackfriars Bridge. Although all traces of the ancient jetties are gone the site is a gold mine of relics from London's past covering the fifteenth to nineteenth centuries. Commonest finds are brass buttons and badges, lead seals, a variety of tokens, and large numbers of coins. This is one of the best sites on which to hunt foreign coins because the old dock was once used by ships from many parts of the world. Chinese, Indian and Egyptian

To banks of Stour and Deben

To Colne, and Mersea Island,
banks of Crouch, Blackwater

Along Grand Junction Canal

To Tilbury, Chadwell, Stanford,
Fobbing, Pitsea, Canvey Island

To Barking Creek,
Dagenham Marshes,
Rainham, Purfleet

To banks of Medway

To creeks around Sheppey

By rail to mid-Sussex   By rail to mid-Kent

coins of the eighteenth and nineteenth centuries have been
found in recent years. London rockhounds, who have to
travel long distances to Britain's mountainous regions for
most of their specimens, can pick up gold coloured cubes of
iron pyrites on this site—reminders of the days when
vessels loaded with coal from south Wales discharged their
cargoes at Blackfriars. The pyrites, often found in coal
mines, were thrown into the river by stevedores as they
unloaded the coal.

Fig. 3 The disposal of Victorian London's refuse.

On the other side of the river, a few yards downstream
from the Mermaid Theatre, lies Queenhithe, another
ancient dock and probably the best site on the river for
relics of London's past. In the reign of Alfred the Great,
Queenhithe was London's most important dock, but its
position above London Bridge caused its decline in later
centuries because large ships could not pass through the

arches of the bridge. It did, however, remain an important mooring point for small river craft until the end of the nineteenth century.

The finds made at Queenhithe by Victorian mudlarks have filled many display cabinets at both the London Museum and the British Museum. They include Saxon and Viking swords and daggers, medieval toys, thousands of coins and tokens, stoneware Bellarmine bottles, lead buttons and seals, clay tobacco pipes, pewter spoons, buckles, badges, rings, brooches, and much more. So many objects have been found that it might seem that the storehouse of relics hidden along the foreshore must be almost exhausted. Yet on any weekend a dozen or more twentieth-century mudlarks can be found at work in the ancient dock and all will make exciting finds before the tide rolls in once more to sift and sort the treasures that still await discovery. On my last visit to Queenhithe I saw a superb eighteenth-century pistol dug out of the mud; my own finds that day included a token dated 1650 and a one-guinea coin weight of William III. Readers hoping for more spectacular finds should note that a hoard of nineteenth-century jewellery lies buried somewhere in the river mud hereabouts. The proceeds of a daring robbery from a jeweller's shop in Cornhill, it was thrown into the river by one of the thieves shortly before his capture. Police divers attempted to recover the loot, but they were unsuccessful.

Visitors to this stretch of foreshore are warned that the mud can be deep and dangerous, especially in the area nearest to Blackfriars Bridge. Searches should be confined to the foreshore in and around the dock where the mud is shallower. The secret of success at Queenhithe is to dig as deeply as possible into the foreshore and to wash the black silt from the bottom of the hole through a sieve to locate small coins and other objects.

Finds similar to those made at Queenhithe can be made on any stretch of foreshore exposed on very low tides between Southwark Bridge and Tower Bridge. The area around London Bridge is also highly productive of Roman coins, though the best search areas near the bridge have been dredged in recent years. Below Tower Bridge modern docks flank the river for several miles and dredging for ship moorings has destroyed much of the tidal foreshore. Many of the areas that remain undredged have been covered by a thick layer of hardcore to prevent movement of unstable mud. Exceptions are at Wapping where finds from the first to the nineteenth centuries can be made and at Greenwich where relics of a long naval history lie beneath the foreshore. At certain times of the year exceptionally low tides expose stretches of undisturbed riverbed between Wapping and Greenwich; readers able to reach them by boat will find rich pickings and few competitors. Tide tables giving information on the heights of all tides can be bought for a few pence from the Port of London Authority.

Essex

The Thames Estuary forms the southern boundary of Essex and on its nothern banks lie some of the best bottle hunting sites in Britain. Vast areas alongside the river were reclaimed in the nineteenth century by dumping household refuse from East London which was loaded into barges near Blackfriars Bridge and carried downriver to creeks and marshes bordering the river between Barking and the sea. Here it was dumped—often to a depth of ten or fifteen feet—to form a barrier against the rising tide and to transform uninhabitable marshes to land suitable for cattle grazing and, later, the many industrial sites that now flank the river.

Barking Creek, a busy waterway for many centuries, was at its most prosperous in the nineteenth-century as one of London's major fishing ports. Its wharves were crowded with vessels landing catches from the Thames, where all manner of fish from salmon to whales once swam; but the fishing was doomed when marshes at Dagenham, Rainham, and Wennington were reclaimed and used by industries which polluted the river. By 1870 the fishing vessels in Barking Creek had been replaced by a vast fleet of refuse barges, and the shellfish which once covered the creek bed were themselves covered by thousands of bottles, pipes and pot lids which fell from the barges during unloading. They

15

Fig. 4 Reeds growing
on a Victorian dump
behind an old sea wall
in Essex.

can be found today by bottle collectors who rake the mud, as can many coins and other nineteenth-century relics.

One of the best-known bottle digging sites in Essex is at Rainham where a huge mound of late Victorian and early twentieth century refuse east of the Ford Motor Company's works is being levelled to provide new sites for industry. This work is likely to take several years to complete and it should continue to present many opportunities for digging acitivity. The entire area for two miles inland from the river from Barking Creek to Purfleet overlies Victorian refuse. Whenever excavations for roadworks, pipelaying, housing, and industrial developments take place new dumps will become accessible. A close watch is kept on this area and regular checks at local council planning offices made by the Essex branch of the British Bottle Collectors Club which has already held group digs here. No doubt many more will take place during the next few years.

By 1880 most of the marshland downriver as far as Purfleet had been reclaimed and London corporations were obliged to seek new sites further eastward. The next large areas suitable for reclamation lay between Tilbury and Canvey Island and it is from this region that most bottle collectors in Essex dig their finds. A newcomer walking the Thames foreshore here might be disappointed by the dumps he discovers. Most are modern and few of the bottles found on the foreshore are worth collecting. The reason for this is that Victorian dumping took place much further inland on what is now good cattle grazing land—at West Tilbury, Chadwell, Stanford, Fobbing and Pitsea—more than a mile from the present foreshore. The heights to which tides rose in Victorian times can be seen from the old flood prevention walls on Fobbing and Pitsea marshes, now surrounded by green fields and grazing cattle, where brackish waters once flowed.

Amateur treasure hunters will find the modern foreshore between Tilbury Fort and Coalhouse Fort worthy of attention. Roman coins in large numbers have been recovered from the riverside and it is believed there was a Roman ferry across the river at this point. Coins, musket balls, badges and buttons from the seventeenth, eighteenth and nineteenth centuries can be found. Further downriver at Leigh-on-Sea is another foreshore that holds Roman coins. In 1769 a hoard was exposed by a cliff fall at Leigh and since then Roman coins have continued to turn up on the beach. Southend is another beach which occasionally produces Roman coins, but detector users visiting the town are advised to hunt nineteenth- and twentieth-century coinage and jewellery if they wish to make a large number of finds. The beach around the pier is most productive. Bottle collectors hoping to find examples used by Southend's Victorian breweries and mineral water makers should join the British Bottle Collectors Club and attend one of the weekend digs organized by the Essex branch at Great Wakering. The site here was used by Southend Corporation from 1880.

The banks of the rivers Crouch, Blackwater and Colne

have yet to be fully explored by bottle dump hunters; but research at London's Guildhall Library has confirmed that large amounts of refuse were also dumped on marshes along these riverbanks in the late Victorian period. Surveys by Essex bottle collectors have revealed glass and pottery fragments and derelict barge moorings at the following locations to which readers hoping to find new sites should direct their attention.

Crouch: Near South Woodham Ferrers.
Two miles downstream from Burn-ham.
On Potton Island on the Roach tributary.

Blackwater: On Osea Island.
East of Tollesbury.
North of Lower Mayland.

Colne: East of Langenhoe.
North of Mersea Island.

Mersea Island and the banks of the Colne and the Black-water are also excellent amateur treasure hunting sites. Roman coins can be found on the foreshore near Mersea Mount and around the ancient landing stage at King's Hard where Saxon, Elizabethan and Victorian coins have also turned up. The Colne riverbed below East Bridge in Colchester contains large numbers of Roman and later coins; Beacon Hard, on the riverside near Fingrinhoe, is another excellent site for Roman and medieval coins; Brightlingsea, near the mouth of the Colne, has an interest-ing beach which produces many Roman finds including complete glass and pottery bottles. The best sites on the Blackwater are at Heybridge where many Roman coins including at least one large hoard have been found between the river and the railway line, and at Bradwell Point where Roman coins and other relics can be found on the foreshore.
The beaches between Brightlingsea and Harwich are the only pebble-collecting sites worthy of mention. Jasper and

Fig. 5 Bottles from Essex.

agate can be found without difficulty, while diligent searches on shingle beaches between Clacton and Walton produce occasional amber and cornelian. The same stretch of coastline holds its share of modern coins and jewellery—to be found after stormy weather on the beaches at Clacton and at Frinton where Roman coins also turn up. Harwich has Roman coins on its beach between Dovercourt and Irlam, while the foreshore inside Harwich harbour is rich in seventeenth-, eighteenth- and nineteenth-century relics. There are several wrecks in the Harwich area accessible at low tide. One of these lies in the mud off Parkeston; it carried a cargo of Dutch clay tobacco pipes and specimens can be found when the tide recedes.

As every experienced amateur treasure hunter knows, hoards of coins and other valuables are most likely to be found near those places where hoards have already been found or where single coins have been unearthed at some time in the past. In 1969 a find made in Essex provided spectacular proof of this rule when a workman on a building site in Colchester dug up an ancient lead casket while cutting a trench on the site of an old chemist's shop. His pick knocked the top off the container and he gazed down on a sparkling hoard of 10,000 silver coins. They were in such fine condition the workman at first thought he had found a hoard of modern sixpences; but later inspection revealed they were thirteenth-century long-cross pennies worth up to £50 each. Several days later, when officials at the local museum checked records on the history of the site, it was learned that in 1920 a lead bucket containing 11,000 short-cross pennies had been found by another workman a few feet from the spot on which the 1969 discovery was made. I take some pride in the fact that I suggested the site as a possible hoard location in an earlier book (*A Fortune Under Your Feet*) written before the second hoard came to light. The following gazetteer of other potential hoard sites in Essex will, I hope, guide a reader of this book to an equally exciting find. Much of the information provided comes from the files of the Essex branch of the British Amateur Treasure Hunting Club, a large and dedicated group of enthusiasts who have carefully researched many sites in the county.

Ashdon: Single Roman coins have been found over a wide area in fields surrounding Barton Hills.

Billericay: Coins of Germanicus, Nero, Trajan, Hadrian and Constantine have been found in Norsey Wood. Gold coins have come to light on Windmill Hill.

Braintree: 3,000 bronze and silver Roman coins were found in the garden of a house owned by Mrs. J. Tabor in 1828. Another large hoard was found in the grounds of

High Garrett House, Bocking, in 1834; a third was discovered during drainlaying at the junction of Sandpit Lane and Rayne Road in 1906.

Brentwood: In 1948 a Roman gold finger ring was found in the garden of Major G. C. Plaistowe, Hillside Walk. A year later two coins of Vespasian were dug up on an allotment garden between North Road and High Street.

Bumpstead: In the nineteenth century a pot containing Roman silver coins was discovered in Ford Meadow, Sturmer. A single gold coin was also found.

Chelmsford: Private garden finds include Roman coins at 3 Goldlay Gardens (rear); 21 Moulsham Street (orchard); 4 Hamlet Road (front); and 54a Mildmay Road (rear).

Chignal Smealy: Roman coins have been found at Matthews Farm.

Chigwell: Single Roman coins have been found over a long period at Woolston Hall.

Colchester: Numerous finds of Roman coins in gardens throughout the town; also many finds made during excavations for air-raid shelters in 1939. Coins of Charles I were found near the cemetery in 1933.

Cressing: Roman coins have been found in Duffus Field, Cressing Temple Farm, and in a field 450 yards south east of Sheepcote Wood.

Danbury: Roman coins have been found in gardens in Riffham's Lane.

Debden: Many Roman bronze coins have been found near Peverel's Wood.

Elmstead: A single gold coin was found in a ploughed field west of the church near Manor House in 1941.

Epping: A bronze statuette six inches tall was found in 1942 near Ambresbury Banks.

Fairstead: Roman coins have been found at Ashwell's Farm near Fuller Street.

Finchingfield: Allotment gardens here have yielded Roman coins.

Gestingthorpe: The fields around Hill Farm contain Roman coins.

Great Canfield: A scatter of Roman coins have been

Fig. 6 A Victorian
purse found in Epping
Forest.

found in the field west of Fitz Johns House.

Great Chesterford: Borough Field has a local reputation of being rich in gold. So far only a few gold coins and some Roman silver objects found.

Great Coggeshall: Roman coins have turned up in Crow Barn Field and Garden Field.

Great Dunmow: Many Roman coins were found in the eighteenth century in a field near the church. Threader's Green has also yielded Roman coins.

Great Horkesley: Roman coins have been found in the garden of the Rose and Crown Hotel, and in the garden of a cottage adjoining the Half Butt Hotel.

Hadleigh: A Roman coin was found some years ago in the garden at 28 Meadow Road.

Halstead: Roman coins have turned up at Locke's Market Garden.

High Easter: Roman coins and other metal objects were found in the gardens of Stagden Cross Villas.

Hornchurch: 400 silver coins of Henry III were found at a depth of eighteen inches in Hornchurch Road, opposite the police station, in 1938.

Ingatestone: In 1921 Roman coins were found on previously uncultivated land at Light Oaks Farm, Mill Green.

Kelvedon: Danish coins were found near the church hall in 1873. Roman coins have turned up in the allotments adjoining Orchard Road.

Lamarsh: Roman coins have been found at Edgar's Farm.

Lawford: Roman coins were found in 1930 in a field 300 yards south-east of Lower Barn.

Leigh: Many Roman coins have turned up in Church Field and Shore Field on Leigh Hall Farm. A number of Roman coins were found in the garden of Hillside House in 1883; more turned up in 1906.

Little Bromley: A Roman gold coin was found at Little Bromley Hall Farm in 1890.

Littlebury: Several Roman coins and rings have been found on Chapel Green. A Roman gold coin was found some years ago in Strawberry Close.

Little Coggeshall: A Roman silver coin turned up south west of Curd Hall several years ago.

Little Dunmow: Roman silver and bronze coins have been found in the sidings at Felsted Railway Station. Two Roman coins have been found in the garden of the cottage near Little Dunmow Priory. Bourchiers Farm, east of Felsted Station, has yielded Roman coins.

Little Thurrock: Roman coins have been found near Hangman's Wood.

Little Waltham: In 1901 a hoard of 180 Roman coins was found in a gravel pit at Sheepcoates Farm.

Little Yeldham: Roman coins have turned up south of Upper Yeldham Hall.

Loughton: In 1908 three boys playing in Monks Wood found a large hoard of damaged jewellery, part of the proceeds of a robbery in Great Yarmouth earlier that year.

Maldon: A Roman gold coin was found in the garden of The Lodge some years ago.

Margaretting: A hoard of Roman coins was found in 1930 near White's Place.

Pleshey: Roman coins have been found in fields at Plesheybury Farm.

Prittlewell: Roman coins were found near the Prittle Brook, Rooks Hill Estate in 1955. A Roman coin turned up recently in the garden of 32 Richmond Drive.

Ramsden Crays: In the nineteenth century a hoard of 1,100 bronze coins was found in a field at Tylde Hall Farm.

Rayleigh: In 1849 a hoard of Roman silver coins was ploughed up in Fishponds Field, White House Farm.

Ridgewell: Roman silver coins have been found over a long period in Great Ashley Field.

Saffron Walden: Two Roman coins were found some years ago in the maze at The Common; Roman coins have been found in the gardens of Walden Place.

Southchurch: The Thorpe Bay area has produced Roman coins over a long period. Roman silver coins have been found at Hamstel Farm.

Stebbing: Many Roman coins have been found in the field south-east of the road to Saling, a quarter of a mile north of Porter's Hall.

Terling: In 1824 a hoard of gold and silver coins together with several gold rings was found at Terling Park Place, one mile west of Hatfield Wick.

Thaxted: A Roman gold earring was found some years ago at Richmond Green.

Thundersley: Roman coins have been found at Dawes Heath.

Tolleshunt D'Arcy: A Roman silver coin was found several years ago in the garden of The Limes, Tiptree.

Vange: A Roman coin was found in a field 400 yards south-east of Merricks Farm in 1957.

Walthamstow: While digging his allotment garden adjoining Higham's Park in 1922 a man found a gold chain and other fragments of jewellery.

Wickhams Bishops: In 1908 a Roman coin was found in a field north of North Hill House.

Witham: A silver coin of St Edmund was found in Temple Meadow near the railway station in 1934; in the same year two James I shillings were found on the edge of a pond at Cressing Temple. Roman coins have turned up in a field at Ivy Chimneys.

Writtle: In 1943 Roman coins were found in a field north of One Bridge.

At a ceremony at High Beech in 1882 Queen Victoria formally opened Epping Forest as a public amenity 'for the enjoyment of the people for all time'. Taking the Queen at her word, Essex amateur treasure hunters have for several years derived much enjoyment from the forest's footpaths and picnic spots where large amounts of Victorian coinage and jewellery can be found with the aid of a metal detector. The best hunting grounds are the sites of the great fairs to which the citizens of East London flocked in the nineteenth century. Most popular was Fairlop Fair, first held in the eighteenth century beneath the shade of the Great Fairlop Oak which stood a mile north-east of Aldborough Hatch near the site of the present Hainault recreation ground. The entire population of Wapping and several other boroughs met there on the first Friday in June from 1725 until 1856 for a roisterous entertainment which so displeased the authorities that they eventually chopped down the tree and enclosed the site. Refusing to accept this denial of their pleasure the crowds simply moved the venue to a new site opposite the old maypole at Barkingside where it was held up to 1900. Popular fairs were also held on Wanstead Flats; in a field opposite the Bald Hind Inn at Chigwell; on a site near the church at Waltham Cross; outside the King's Head at Chigwell; at Abridge Green near Lambourne; and in a field near the Roebuck Inn at Buckhurst Hill.

Kent

Kent's coastline from Whitstable to Dungeness can be profitably searched for pebbles of jasper, agate, cornelian, quartzite and chalcedony. The holiday resorts of Herne Bay, Margate, Broadstairs, Ramsgate, Deal and Folkestone all have shingle beaches within a few miles where good specimens can be found by diligent pebble hunters. Beaches at Ramsgate, Margate and Broadstairs are also excellent locations on which to hunt nineteenth-century coins and jewellery; they were among the first to be patronized by day trippers after 1850 when railway links with the capital made seaside holidays possible for thousands of Londoners. The foreshore at Deal has Roman as well as Victorian coins.

The sleepy village of Pegwell Bay, a few miles south of Ramsgate, holds an undiscovered fortune in coloured pot lids. The refuse dump used by the village from 1850 to 1880 has yet to be located by diggers; when it is they will almost certainly find thousands of coloured lids discarded by the shrimp paste makers of the village when the industry collapsed in the late Victorian period. For nearly thirty years factories at Pegwell packaged their shrimp paste in pots with coloured lids made by F. & R. Pratt & Co. of Fenton and other famous pot lid makers. The paste was sold throughout Britain, though the main markets were in seaside resorts along the south coast and in London's upper-class grocery shops where customers were prepared to pay extravagant prices for it because the containers were so attractive. By 1880 shrimp paste was being made much more cheaply at large factories in London and coloured paper labels, which could be made for a fraction of the cost of underglaze transfers, proved equally attractive to customers. The shrimping grounds around Ramsgate had by this time become over-fished and the Pegwell Bay industry, unable to compete with London rivals, died almost overnight—leaving thousands of worthless pots to be relegated to the local refuse dump.

Many Pegwell Bay lids have already been found by Kent's dump diggers on marshland sites between Gillingham and Sittingbourne where Victorian London's refuse was dumped when the volume proved too great for the Essex marshes. The best sites discovered so far lie along the creeks around Milton Regis and Lower Halstow where

group digs organized by the Kent branch of the British Bottle Collectors Club have been most successful. Other towns in Kent where dumps are being excavated include Canterbury, Herne Bay, Whitstable and Tonbridge, where local Victorian refuse has produced excellent finds; and at Sittingbourne and Faversham, where more London refuse has come to light. Research evidence suggests Chetney Marshes, the low-lying land around Conyer, and the area around Graveney as sites where more large dumps might be found.

Much London refuse taken to Kent marshes was carried by barge, but large amounts also went by rail to the Long-field and Meopham areas. At the time of writing these vast Victorian dumps have not been located. Nor has the Medway estuary been extensively explored by bottle collectors. In 1973 I took part in a search of the Thames and Medway foreshores from Gravesend to Hoo during which interesting

Fig. 7 The River Medway, a great river for bottle dump hunters and amateur treasure hunters.

27

Fig. 8 Pot lids from
dumps on the Medway
estuary.

sites were located near Cliffe, Allhallows, and at Hoo. The
foreshores hereabouts are littered with broken Codd's,
ginger beers, and clay tobacco pipes—all from London. No
doubt many of the islands in the Medway estuary were also
used as convenient sites on which to dump London's
enormous amounts of nineteenth-century rubbish.

Amateur treasure hunters will also find the Medway
foreshores around Rochester and Chatham excellent sites on
which to locate coins and relics from the first to the nineteenth centuries. Many Roman finds have been made in and
around Chatham dockyard and near the mouth of the river
on the Isle of Grain. The Thames foreshore opposite Tilbury
is another excellent site for coins and relics of all periods.

Kent has its share of buried treasure sites. In 1907 nine
Celtic gold bracelets were found by workmen employed by
the Crayford Land, Brick, and Sand Company in a sandpit
at Crayford—only a few hundred yards from the spot where
eight similar bracelets were dug up one year earlier. In 1934

28

another group of workmen dug up a pot containing 360 Roman silver and bronze coins in Shenwood Road, St Mary Cray, close to the location of a single coin find a few days before. Another Roman hoard turned up in Church Street, Maidstone in 1935, and in 1941 a pot of gold coins was dug out of the front garden at Chantry Cottage, Bredgar. A few weeks later a platoon of Home Guards digging practice trenches at Northfield found a small hoard of coins dated 1809.

A much larger hoard containing more than 5,000 Roman coins was ploughed up in 1959 by a tractor driver working in a field at Hallingbourne near Maidstone. The ploughshare broke the pot containing the hoard and the coins were scattered across the field. In 1967 another Maidstone tractor driver suddenly found himself £5,000 richer when a Saxon gold cross he had ploughed up in a field at Thurnham was valued at that figure during the subsequent Treasure Trove inquest. No doubt other Kentish farmworkers and amateur treasure hunters will discover much more beneath the county's soil during the next few years.

Middlesex and north London

This area offers amateur treasure hunters first-class parks, commons and open spaces on which to use detectors, and the most popular site is undoubtedly Hampstead Heath where thousands of antique coins and other interesting relics have been found by coinshooters. In 1973 an enthusiast using an inexpensive detector located a hoard of silverware here, and several Victorian purses stuffed with coins in exceptionally good condition have also been found in recent months. Hampstead Heath Fair, to which Londoners flocked in their thousands during the nineteenth century, was held on land adjoining East Heath Road and it is from this area that many of the best finds have come.

In the eastern part of this area, near the borders with Essex and Hertfordshire, there was once a vast tract of forest land known as Enfield Chase; a royal hunting ground and a refuge for thousands of highwaymen, footpads and other outlaws for centuries. Numerous hoards of robbery loot were certainly buried here in the past and some must

Fig. 9 Every one of these silver threepenny pieces was found on Hampstead Heath.

still await discovery in the remnants of the forest which survive today as open spaces. These include Hadley Wood, Hadley Common, and Trent Park, all sites where excellent single coin finds can be made.

An equally impressive and notorious stretch of natural vegetation once covered the western borders of Middlesex. This was Hounslow Heath, now almost completely lost beneath housing estates, roads, and the runways of London Airport, but known as late as 1850 as 'a nursery for thieves and the scene of many murders and robberies'. What little remains of the original heath is now incorporated in Bushey Park which adjoins Hampton Court. Several years ago a friend of mine found a highwayman's pistol and some coins hidden at the base of a tree here. Many other finds have been made including coins, jewellery, musket balls, daggers and swords—relics of the days when no traveller on the Bath Road was safe from the attention of the bands of rogues and ruffians who called Hounslow Heath their home. Other parks and commons on which good finds have been made by coinshooters include Stanmore Common, Highgate Wood, Osterley Park, Ealing Common, Old Oak Common and Marble Hill Park.

Several interesting finds of Roman coins have been made in the Harrow area. Thirteen bronze coins were dug up a few years ago in the garden of 137a Pinner Road; a hoard of 50 Roman silver coins was found on Stanmore Common in 1781; and many Roman coins including gold specimens have been found in Money Dell near Bentley Priory, Harrow Weald. From Hornsey have come three hoards—a pot of bronze coins found in the grounds of the Priory, Shepherd's Hill Road; a small hoard found in a garden in Barrenger Road; and a hoard of 650 Roman silver and bronze coins dug up in 1928 by a boy aged fourteen in his front garden at 104 Cranley Gardens, Muswell Hill. Roman coin finds in Edmonton include a number found in the garden of 7 Forest Road in 1943, and a single silver coin dug up some years ago at 421 Monmouth Road. Many Roman coins have also been found in and around Brentford, but the most interesting find in the town was made several years ago when a man digging in his allotment garden turned up a vase containing James I and Charles I coins which were probably hidden when Royalist forces overran the district after the Battle of Brentford during the Civil War.

It is from the borders of Middlesex a little more than a mile from West Drayton that some of the best finds made by Britain's dump diggers have come. Here, on a branch of the Grand Junction Canal, lies the Iver dump from which hundreds of collectors have dug thousands of valuable bottles, pot lids, pipes and dolls' heads since the dump was discovered in 1972. During that first bonanza year any digger who pushed a fork into the ground on this site could expect to find at least two pot lids, half a dozen Hamilton's, and probably a sealed wine bottle for every cubic yard of earth he turned over. Alas, pickings are much leaner nowadays, but good finds of dolls' heads, pipe bowls and small bottles missed in the excitement of those first digs can still be made by those prepared to search carefully.

Most of West London's nineteenth-century refuse was dumped along the banks of the Grand Junction Canal which flows through Uxbridge, Cowley, West Drayton and Southall before joining the River Brent to reach the Thames at Brentford. Few searches for undiscovered dumps along its banks have yet been made because most diggers have concentrated their efforts on the Iver site where until quite recently any collector could obtain all the specimens he desired. Soon that site will become exhausted and diggers will begin to explore the canal in the hope of finding one of the many equally productive dumps that must lie somewhere between Brentford and Uxbridge. Any reader who finds the time to take a slow trip by barge or small boat along this stretch of waterway and who probes every clump of nettles and elders along the route will certainly discover such a dump and start the second bonanza.

2 The South Coast

The main holiday beaches of the Sussex coast—Hastings, Eastbourne, Brighton and Bognor—offer detector users excellent sport. They are rich in modern coinage and jewellery with a fair amount of Victorian and earlier coins thrown in for good measure. On Hastings beach finds of eighteenth-century Dutch coins have recently been made; they probably come from the wreck of the Dutch ship *Amsterdam* which lies buried in the sand exposed at low tide. Eastwards from Hastings amateur treasure hunters searching the Winchelsea beach and the area around Rye Harbour have come up with finds from the thirteenth to the eighteenth century. The ancient town of Old Winchelsea was destroyed in 1250 when a violent storm battered the town's walls and more than three hundred houses were swallowed by the waves. At Rye the sea has slowly receded and this once busy port has been left high and dry. In the seventeenth and eighteenth centuries the marshlands thus created provided haunts and hideaways for many smuggling gangs who brought in large amounts of bullion and armaments for Charles I during the Civil War. In the eighteenth century, when much of the contraband was French brandy, tobacco and tea, smuggling was the most important industry on this coast.

Eastbourne's beaches from the town to Beachy Head should be searched by those seeking Victorian coins, while beaches to the east of the town produce largely modern finds. Further eastwards, around Pevensey Bay, much earlier coins and relics await discovery The Romans had an important fortress here built on a peninsula reaching into the sea. It guarded a town which continued to thrive as a port until the Middle Ages when the sea receded and left Pevensey stranded four miles inland. The area between the Norman castle and the modern coastline holds many excellent finds.

Seaford and Newhaven, to the west of Beachy Head, were important medieval ports. At that time the Ouse entered the sea close to Seaford and large ships could anchor at the town's wharves. The river was a busy thorough-fare and many vessels sailed upstream as far as Lewes. Today coins of all periods can be found on the tidal banks of this river, especially at Lewes where the area around the bridge is highly productive at low tide.

Brighton was Britain's first seaside resort and the London to Brighton railway line the first to be built for the sole purpose of carrying holiday travellers. Long before it opened in 1841 Brighton was patronized by London's fashionable society who went there either for a curative dip in the sea or to board a cross-Channel packet boat on a journey to Paris. A pier was built at Brighton in 1823 to enable passengers to embark directly onto the boats from their coaches; it was destroyed during a storm in 1896, but the site on which it stood opposite Marine Parade is an excellent location for nineteenth-century coins. This spot, like many others on the south coast, gives up its best finds after rough seas have pounded the beach and disturbed the sand and shingle to bring lost coins and jewellery nearer to the surface. Holiday visitors who do not have the time to wait for a storm to break should dig the beach to a depth of two feet and use their detectors on the material turned over. The beach around West Pier and opposite Kingsway is also highly productive of Victorian relics when worked in this way.

Twenty miles inland from Brighton lies Horsham, a classic coinshooting town for those who require a diversion from beach treasure hunting. From the mid-sixteenth-century until 1843 when a new county gaol was built at Lewes the county assizes were held at Horsham or at East Grinstead. During Horsham's assize week thousands of visitors poured in and many of them camped on the great common north of the town where prisoners condemned to death were publicly hanged. A number of smuggling gangs were dealt with in this way up to 1820, but after that date the crowds had to content themselves with the 'enter-tainment' provided by whip, stocks and pillory. Many coins and other fascinating relics lost by these spectators can be found on the site by those equipped with sensitive detectors.

34

Fig. 10 Rare 'Odol'
bottles from a Sussex
bottle dump.

Returning to the coast, most of the finds to be made between Bognor and Selsey are modern, though the sea-front at Bognor produces some Victorian coins. West of Selsey Bill between the town and East Wittering is a stretch of coastline rich in coins and relics of the Celtic and Roman periods. There was a Celtic settlement, now washed away by the sea, on this foreshore, and much Roman activity in the area. In 1925 a lady walking along the beach here picked up a Celtic gold bracelet weighing almost half a pound. Many Roman finds have also been made in Chichester Harbour.

35

Pebble collectors will find the beaches around Selsey Bill excellent hunting grounds for quartzite and chalcedony, while shingle beds between Bognor and Brighton occasionally produce interesting specimens of amber when searched immediately after stormy weather. Pebble hunters working the area between Brighton and Hastings should find agate, quartzite and cornelian. Nodules of marcasite can also be found in the chalk cliffs around Beachy Head.

Bottle collecting is a popular hobby in Sussex, but at present the majority of sites on which digging takes place are small village dumps excavated by groups of two or three diggers. The exception is a large woodland site on the outskirts of Hastings on which several digs organized by the Sussex branch of the British Bottle Collectors Club have taken place. Excellent finds including pot lids and many decorated pipe bowls have been found here.

It is known that large amounts of refuse from south London were taken by rail to dumps in mid-Sussex during the period 1900–20, but these dumps have not yet been found. They probably lie between Crawley and Haywards Heath on branches off the main London to Brighton line. Research has confirmed that railway waggons carrying the rubbish returned to London loaded with bricks, an indication that the dumping grounds were almost certainly clay pits near brickyards. Earlier dumps containing Victorian refuse from Bognor, Brighton, Eastbourne and Hastings await discovery on the banks of disused canals in the county. Barges on the Portsmouth–Arun canal, which closed before 1880, carried refuse from Bognor to sites near Chichester Harbour, and boats loaded with refuse from Brighton and Eastbourne converged on the canalized Ouse to reach dumps near Lewes. In the eastern part of the county, barges collected refuse from Hastings and carried it to marshes around Rye Harbour and to pits along the Rother Navigation.

Members of the county's most active treasure hunting club—Sussex Treasure Hunters—have made exciting finds during the past few years including a hoard of more than 5,000 Roman coins and some valuable sixteenth-century

coins discovered when a derelict cottage was searched. The
following notes culled from a club member's research files
indicate that prospects of major treasure finds in Sussex during
the next few years are extremely good. In 1929 large numbers
of Roman coins were found two miles south-east of Pul-
borough close to the West Sussex Golf Club. Three years later
a man digging his garden at Fish Lane, Selsey unearthed a pot
containing more than 1,000 Roman silver coins. In the
following year a number of silver coins of Edward I were
dug up in East Grinstead Churchyard, and in 1937 silver
coins of Edward VI minted in 1550 were found near
North Chapel House adjoining the railway station at
Horsham. One of the county's most interesting treasure
stories comes from Lewes. In 1934 a number of Tudor coins
were picked up in a field at Loughton on the outskirts of

Lewes by a farm labourer. Twenty-five years later a bright-eyed schoolboy working in the same field spotted several pieces of a broken urn. He had heard the story of the earlier find so he took a closer look—and found 600 half crowns of the late Tudor and early Stuart period.

Hampshire Amateur treasure hunters entering Hampshire along the coast road from Sussex will reach Hayling Island within a few minutes of crossing the county border. Here is a truly fascinating treasure site that has lured hundreds of experienced detector users from all parts of Britain during the past few years. The majority come to hunt Elizabethan silver coins for which Hayling Island's beaches are famous, but some are seeking more spectacular finds including at least one treasure chest lost somewhere on the foreshore.

It was in the summer of 1972 that modern beachcombers became seriously interested in Hayling Island when a large number of gold and silver coins, including many dating back to the reign of Elizabeth I and in excellent condition, began to turn up in shingle beds around the island disturbed during a series of severe storms. Detector users on holiday at Hayling that year made excellent finds and those who took the trouble to enquire where all those coins might have come from heard colourful tales of smuggling, wrecking and piracy on the island four or five hundred years ago. They also heard a strange story about a local fisherman who had found a brass box containing a hoard of Elizabethan coins while fishing from the beach in 1966. After bitter disputes with his relatives about sharing the find this man threw the box and its contents back into the sea. Reports on the number of coins the box contained vary from seventy to more than one hundred; if they were in similar condition to some of those found in 1972 they could now be worth up to £200 each!

The foreshores and beaches of Portsmouth Harbour, the rivers flowing into Southampton Water, and the coast of the Isle of Wight also have excellent sites for beachcombing and coinshooting. Portsmouth Harbour is rich in naval relics; from inside the harbour and from sites near Spithead have come bronze cannon, anchors, swords, brass buttons and badges, ships' fittings, and many seventeenth- and eighteenth-century coins. In Gurnard Bay on the Isle of Wight Roman coins are washed from the cliffs and can be picked up on the beach at low tide. Excellent coins and other relics of the eighteenth and nineteenth centuries can be raked from the River Hamble above Burlesdon Bridge, and Roman finds can be made by using similar techniques above Northam Bridge on the Itchen. At Nursling on the east bank of the Test many Roman silver and bronze coins together with items of Roman jewellery were found in the late nineteenth-century when gravel along the riverbank was dug up for ballast.

The Hampshire coast beyond Southampton Water is less productive, but excellent finds of modern coins and jewellery have been made by beachcombers and detector users on Bournemouth's golden sands. Most spectacular was the hoard of 4,000 gold, silver and bronze coins dug up in 1914. Sadly, some of the most interesting search areas on this site have been covered by a modern rubbish dump, but the foreshores hereabouts are worth searching.

There are many inland sites in Hampshire where Roman coins can be found by detector users. The fields around Andover in the northern part of the county are highly productive. At Appleshaw coins have turned up in large numbers in Great Copse and Chapel Copse; a hoard was found some years ago in Minster Field, Abbott's Ann, and many single coins have also been located in Harewood Forest south east of Andover.

Mitcheldever Wood, eight miles north-east of Winchester, produced a hoard of 1,400 coins in 1844. A Roman road runs through the wood and the hoard was found very close to it. Several other woods and copses in Hampshire have turned out to hold valuable finds—Barton Wood, I.O.W., produced a large hoard in 1833; Norley Wood near Lymington was the scene of a large find in the late nineteenth century; many single coins have been discovered in College Wood, Popham, and in Little Lippen Wood on the outskirts of West Meon; and both West Wood and Cowdown

Copse near Farley Mount, Sparsholt, have produced many coins.

The treasure-hunting rule that hoards turn up where hoards have already been found was shown to be true in Hampshire in 1967 when a woman working on an archaeological site at Rockbourne found a pot containing 7,707 Roman coins. In 1893 a pot containing 4,020 coins was found by a farm labourer in a nearby field. Even more spectacular was the series of finds made in the eighteenth and nineteenth centuries at Selborne, a few miles south-east of Alton. In the summer of 1741 a pond in the grounds of Blackmore House, Selborne, dried up and several thousand coins which appeared to have once been contained in a sack were found in the mud. Three years later the pond dried up once again and boys playing there pulled out a large urn filled with coins. More than a century later, in 1867, a second urn containing 100 silver coins was found. Even then this fascinating site had not given up all its treasures. In 1873 two very large urns were dug up just two hundred yards from the pond. The number of coins they contained totalled 29,802—one of the largest finds ever made in Britain.

My favourite treasure story from Hampshire is that of a small boy aged four who was playing near a hollow pear tree in the garden of his home at Winston Avenue, Tadley, near Basingstoke when he found a rusty tin containing 21 guineas and half-guineas of George III. That happened as recently as 1963, but thirty-seven years earlier three slightly older children who also came from Basingstoke dug up a jar full of gold coins in a roadside embankment on the outskirts of the town.

Much of Hampshire's coastline is taken up by large and muddy natural harbours and by wide river estuaries which provide poor prospects for pebble collectors. Beaches on the western side of the Isle of Wight offer some hopes of finding jasper or agate, and specimens of amber are occasionally washed up on the eastern beaches of the island; but pebble hunters looking for good finds are advised to take their holidays further westward in Dorset and Devon—

Fig. 12 Foreign bottles
from Southampton
Harbour.

unless they are also keen bottle collectors. A number of
small but highly productive bottle dumps have been located
in steep coastal valleys, or chines, on the Isle of Wight and
in the Bournemouth area, and good bottle finds have also
been made in the muddy parts of Portsmouth Harbour and

Fig. 13 (*above*) Finds from riversides in Hampshire.

Fig. 14 (*right*) Pot lid from a Hampshire dump.

Langston Harbour. The largest dumps in Hampshire are to be found on former marshland on the western shores of Southampton Water and on the outskirts of Totton. Much Victorian refuse from Southampton and Portsmouth was also dumped in chalk quarries along the banks of the Andover Canal. In Andover there is an interesting site on which group digs organized by the Hampshire branch of the British Collectors Club take place. It lies alongside the River Anton beneath former allotments and it contains excellent bottles, pipes, and pot lids from the 1890s.

Shingle beaches on the Dorset coast hold an interesting **Dorset** selection of pebbles including quartzite, chalcedony, agate and cornelian. There are good collecting areas around Lyme Regis and in the rocky bays between Weymouth and Swanage where Purbeck marble and Kimmeridge shale, both easy to shape and polish, can also be found. Disused stone quarries on Portland are worth exploring.

Known bottle collecting sites in the county are limited to dumps near Poole, Wareham and Swanage, but there are hundreds of villages in the county where experienced diggers should find small Victorian dumps in local woods or on nearby waste ground. The largest dumps yet found in the county are located around the shores of Poole Harbour between Hamworthy and Studland.

Dorset is treasure hunting country with everything from highly productive coinshooting sites to locations on which large hoards have already been discovered or are believed to await discovery; few amateur treasure hunters taking holidays in Dorset should return home without excellent finds. The best site is undoubtedly Chesil Beach between Abbotsbury and Portland, a graveyard for ships driven ashore during the last two thousand years. In 1971 a treasure hunter who worked the beach with a detector during a severe storm found enough coins to fill a suitcase; he also saw the wooden skeleton of a ship exposed when breaking waves swept away a huge mound of pebbles. On visiting the spot the following day when the storm had subsided he found that the vessel had disappeared once again under a

43

newly formed bank of shingle.

Numerous seventeenth- and eighteenth-century coins have been found here. Many are covered by a coating of black tar which makes them appear quite uninteresting; but when the tar is removed they are seen to be in excellent condition. Roman coins which turn up on the beach about one mile west of Portland also have this protective coating. They are thought to come from the wreck of a Roman vessel lost on Chesil Beach almost two thousand years ago. There is an unconfirmed story of a local beachcomber who is said to find ingots of silver somewhere on the beach after violent winter storms. The last time this tale was told to me he was said to have found a total of seventeen ingots in as many years.

Large numbers of coins from all periods have been found on Weymouth beaches. On the outskirts of the town at Jordan Hill, Preston is a site which has produced at least two Roman hoards. A pot containing several hundred silver coins was dug up in 1812 and a second pot containing 4,400 bronze coins was found in 1928. Since then large numbers of single coins—probably from a third hoard—have been discovered here. An even more spectacular find was made five miles away at Dorchester in 1936 when workmen digging foundations for Marks and Spencers' store in the High Street found a pot and a wide dish containing a total of 22,000 Roman coins. Other interesting sites in the county include:

Hamworthy: Celtic and Roman coins have been found on the harbour shore.

Wareham: Numerous coins and relics have turned up in the silted harbour; Roman coins are also dug up in the gardens of houses in Mill Lane, Cow Lane, and South Street.

Sherborne: Fields bordering Pinfold Lane, Castleton, one and a half miles north-west of Sherborne Abbey have produced Celtic and Roman coins.

Wynford Eagle: A number of Roman coins were found several years ago in a bank of earth south-west of Manor Farm.

44

Iwerne Minster: Roman coins have turned up near Park House Farm.

Shaftesbury: Roman coins have been found on Barton Hill.

Charlton Marshall: Allotment gardens here produce Roman coins.

Okeford Fitzpaine: A hoard of 80 Celtic silver coins was found near a chalk pit south of the village in 1753. Another hoard was discovered on the same spot in 1788.

Charminster: Several Roman coins were found in 1960 in Walls Field.

Fifehead Neville: In 1902 a hoard of Roman jewellery and some coins was found thirty yards east of the River Divelish and north of Fifehead Mill.

Hanford: A hoard of Roman coins was discovered on Great Bourne Hill in 1860.

Poole: In 1833 a scatter of Roman bronze coins was found on the surface of Turlin Moor Meadow; a few days later a broken pot containing 300 coins was dug up. A second hoard of 1,000 silver coins was found in the meadow in 1930. In 1936 a hoard was found in allotment gardens at Baiter.

3 South-West England

The granite rocks of Devon provide rockhounds with numerous sites where excellent mineral specimens can be found. There are many abandoned mines with spoil heaps now colonized by brambles, nettles, and weeds on which it is possible to dig up fine crystals of clear quartz, amethyst, and other prizes. They may also be looked for in cliffs around the coast and on many of Devon's beaches where, even though collectors have searched for generations, it is still possible to make worthwhile finds.

Devon

On southern beaches between Lyme Regis and Exmouth, agate, sard, cornelian and potato stones lined with rock crystal and amethyst can be found. Budleigh Salterton is noted for its agate pebbles—especially those from Ladram Bay—and Sidmouth's beaches hold good specimens of clear quartz. Further inland, mines and quarries on the Blackdown Hills are worth exploring for agate, jasper and wood opal. The streams of the Exe valley between Tiverton and Exeter are good sites on which to find specimens by raking gravels and pebbles from the water. South west of Exeter the bleak plateau of Dartmoor, which rises to a height of two thousand feet, is broken by several streams in the Bovey Tracey area where apatite, citrine and rock crystal can be found. On higher ground near Lustleigh abandoned mines provide spoil heaps where beryl and garnet await discovery. Agate and chalcedony can also be found in spoil heaps near Haytor Down.

The popular beaches around Torquay are well-known pebble hunting locations where agate, jasper, cornelian and citrine can all be picked up at low tide. More adventurous souls who penetrate the wilds of Dartmoor inland from Torquay will find excellent locations around Buckfastleigh. Malachite can be found near old mine workings here; it is also found with fluorite in the Buckland area north-east of Ashburton. Ivybridge, south-west of Buckfastleigh, is noted for its jasper.

On the northern edge of Dartmoor good sites are located close to the main road from Exeter to Okehampton. There are several abandoned mines at Sticklepath and Ramsley where garnet, citrine and rock crystal lie beneath overgrown spoil heaps. Mining was also formerly carried out on the western side of Dartmoor in the Milton Abbot and Tavistock districts. Here finds of rhodonite, jasper and garnet await discovery, especially near North Brentor. Very little mining has been carried out in the central regions of Dartmoor where there are no roads and which can only be reached on foot. Rockhounds who have ventured into these regions report good finds from stream banks and around rock outcrops.

The North Devon coast is less productive of semi-precious pebbles, though beaches around Ilfracombe and Bideford are worth exploring. Silver mining was formerly carried out at Combe Martin where good specimens of marcasite and malachite can be found. Stream beds on Exmoor can be profitably searched for a variety of colourful pebbles.

It is an excellent plan to combine rockhounding expeditions in Devon with searches for Victorian refuse dumps. Most of the former mining villages and hamlets close to present-day rockhounding sites had quite large populations in the late nineteenth-century when profitable amounts of ore were being brought to the surface. It was not uncommon for a two-bedroom cottage to have a dozen or more itinerant mine workers as lodgers who slept three or four to a bed and who consumed large quantities of bottled beer, spirits and quack medicines. Although much refuse was thrown into disused mine shafts village dumps were often quite large when the houses lay some distance from the workings. Sites can be located by looking for nettle patches and clumps of elders at the rear of remaining houses.

Some towns on the coast disposed of their refuse by tipping into depressions on neighbouring cliffs. Those situated on rivers—notably Exmouth, Exeter, Teignmouth, Newton Abbot, Dartmouth, Plymouth, Bideford and Barnstaple—loaded refuse onto boats and barges and carried it to sites alongside the local river where it was spread across fields and ploughed into the ground. At Bude

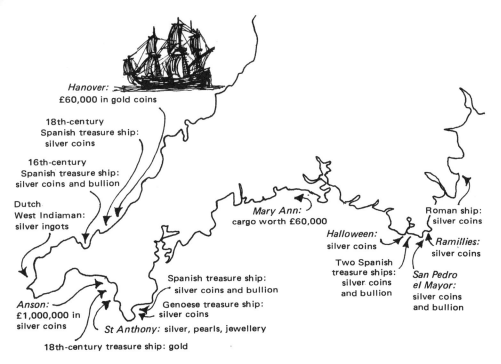

Hanover: £60,000 in gold coins

18th-century Spanish treasure ship: silver coins

16th-century Spanish treasure ship: silver coins and bullion

Dutch West Indiaman: silver ingots

Mary Ann: cargo worth £60,000

Roman ship: silver coins

Halloween: silver coins

Ramillies: silver coins

Two Spanish treasure ships: silver coins and bullion

San Pedro el Mayor: silver coins and bullion

Spanish treasure ship: silver coins and bullion

Genoese treasure ship: silver coins

Anson: £1,000,000 in silver coins

St Anthony: silver, pearls, jewellery

18th-century treasure ship: gold

and Tiverton disused canals provided convenient dumping grounds for late nineteenth-century refuse. Innumerable worked-out quarries throughout the county have also been used as dumps. Any abandoned quarry where nettles and elders grow profusely should be investigated as possible Victorian refuse sites.

Although Devon's seaside resorts now count their summer visitors in tens of thousands, most were sleepy fishing villages in the nineteenth century. For this reason detector users who search popular beaches find few Victorian coins. The best seashore finds are made by those who seek coins and relics from the numerous wrecks around Devon's rocky coastline. These vessels cast up onto the shore a fascinating assortment of doubloons, pieces-of-eight, and other romantic objects including cannon and ships' fittings. True, they are considerably more difficult to find than are the modern fifty-pence pieces which litter popular beaches; but the thrill of finding a relic from a genuine treasure ship more than repays the many hours spent combing the shoreline with a detector.

Fig. 16 Treasure wrecks on the south-west coast.

49

Almost any stretch of coastline in Devon has wrecks lying a little distance offshore, but the best hunting grounds are between Bigbury Bay and Start Bay in the south. It was in this area that the Armada vessel *San Pedro el Mayor* sank in 1588 after circumnavigating Britain following the Spanish defeat in the Channel. She was blown back up the Channel because most of her crew were dead or dying from exposure and battle wounds; there were not enough fit men aboard to steer her to the safety of Spain. Instead she was smashed to matchwood in Hope Cove—where many silver coins from her treasure chests have been picked up on the beach. Two centuries later, in 1760, it was a large British ship, *Ramillies* that went down with six hundred of her crew on the same coast between Hope Cove and Bolt Head. Several of her ninety cannon have been found together with many silver coins. The site of the wreck is known locally as Ramillies Cove.

In nearby Sewer Mill Cove, close to Bolt Head, the wreck of a great tea clipper, *Halloween*, lies in the sand. Excellent coin finds have been made here by detector users who have searched the beach during stormy weather. On the other side of the entrance to Salcombe harbour, just inside Gammon Head, is the spot where two Spanish ships were lost in the seventeenth century. Many doubloons were picked up here in 1891 by beachcombers who reported seeing the timbers of several wrecks on the same beach. In March of that year a terrible blizzard had wrecked hundreds of ships around Britain's coastline and it is known that a steamship, a barque, and two schooners were lost within seven hours between Gammon Head and Start Point. Further north, at Berry Head near Brixham, Roman coins thought to come from an ancient wreck have been found. One of the caves beneath Berry Head is said to hold a treasure hidden by eighteenth-century smugglers.

On the North Devon coast the best hunting areas are found around Ilfracombe. Many seventeenth- and eighteenth-century coins have been located at Baggy Point and at Bull Point where numerous shipwrecks occurred before the lighthouse was built in 1879. In Rapparee Cove a ship taken as a prize after an engagement with the French during the Napoleonic Wars was driven ashore and totally wrecked. Coins and human bones have been found on the beach in the past.

Large numbers of lost coins from all periods have been found in the harbours of Exmouth and Exeter. In the north Ilfracombe's harbour and beaches also produce good finds. There is a local tradition that treasure is buried beneath the foundations of the Manor House near Berrynarbor Church, Ilfracombe, and that hidden gold awaits discovery in the hills and valleys around Combe Martin. It is said to have been hidden by a gang of outlaws who terrorized the district several hundred years ago. In 1973 a party of London amateur treasure hunters visited this area in the hope of finding treasure. The hoard eluded them but excellent finds of seventeenth- and eighteenth-century coins were made. The same group also had much success in Plymouth Harbour where many relics were recovered, though their good fortune failed to match that of a tramp who searched a Plymouth rubbish dump in 1931 in the hope of finding a decent pair of boots. Inside one of the boots he examined was a small envelope; it contained a diamond ring, a pair of gold ear-rings, and a heavy gold necklace.

Cornwall

There are at least as many wrecks around Cornwall's coastline as there are deserted tin mines on its moors. In the days of sail when navigational aids were poor a vessel had to sight land in order to fix its position. This involved sailing very close inshore, especially in bad weather when visibility was at its poorest, and it was the rocky coast of Cornwall that sea captains entering the Channel first encountered. As a result numerous vessels foundered off its dangerous head-lands or were driven ashore by treacherous winds. Many fine ships which might have escaped disaster were lured onto the rocks by lanterns cunningly placed by Cornwall's professional wreckers. These rascals regarded all vessels cast upon Cornish shores as gifts from the gods and they were eager to help the gods in deciding the fate of any ship caught in a storm by showing false lights to confuse the

Fig. 17 (*above left*) Cornish mine—outside.

Fig. 18 (*above right*) Cornish mine—inside.

unfortunate sailors. Many kegs of brandy or handfuls of Spanish doubloons found their way to Cornish cottages in this way and it is for this reason that hundreds of wreck locations are accurately known by local people whose ancestors made a good living from them. The following brief survey of wrecks on the county's coast gives some idea of the vast amounts of coinage, bronze cannon, gold and silver ingots, and rich jewellery yet to be found.

Plymouth South to Rame Head: Large number of warships and merchantmen have gone down in this area. In 1691 two men-of-war were blown ashore in Plymouth Sound. *Conqueror* was wrecked on Drake's Island in 1760; two years later a dozen warships and merchantmen were wrecked in the Sound by a great storm. There were also many losses here in 1817 and 1823, but the worst disaster occurred in October 1824 when twenty-five ships were driven ashore and wrecked. At least a dozen more were to go down before the breakwater was built in 1841. Rame Head continued to claim victims, including the 29-gunner *Cossack* in 1854.

Whitesand Bay and Looe: Losses in this area include the brig *Rose* in 1809, the *Mary Ann* in 1810 (cargo worth £60,000), the sloop *Friend's Endeavour* in 1811, the brig *Harmonie* in 1824, the schooner *Jane* in 1827, the cargo ship *Konisberg* in 1834, the Dutch East Indiaman *Yonge Willem* in 1841, the barque *Duke of Clarence* in 1846, and many more.

St Austell Bay: *Drydens* in 1865, *Wearmouth* the same year, *Girondin* two years later, *Douro* in 1872, *Cecile Caroline* in 1880, and dozens more.

Falmouth Bay: In 1792 the 36-gun frigate *Briel*, in 1811 the 36-gun frigate *Franchise* and the 18-gun sloop *Primrose*. Three hundred lives were lost when the *John and Jane* sank in the same year. Many modern wrecks also recorded in this area.

The Manacles area: More than 100 ships have been wrecked off The Manacles. Two ships sank in a single night during a storm in 1809 with a loss of over one hundred lives. In 1855 the barque *John* was driven ashore and one hundred and twenty passengers and crew were drowned.

The Lizard: More vessels have been wrecked on this most southerly point of the British coast than have been lost anywhere else around these islands. In 1619 a Spanish treasure ship was driven ashore in the Polpeor Cove area. She carried large amounts of silver bullion. Some fifty years later a Genoese treasure ship went down off the Bumble Rock. Other large vessels lost include *Royal Anne* in 1720, *Xanthus* in 1841, *Isabella* in 1850 and *Montana* in 1897.

West of The Lizard: In 1526 the *St Anthony*, a Portuguese ship owned by King John III, was driven ashore near Gunwalloe. Her cargo included silver, pearls, jewels, candlesticks and guns. In the 1780s another treasure ship was wrecked in the same area. This vessel was carrying several tons of gold coins and a number of attempts have been made to recover the treasure. In 1845 a dam was erected across the gully in which the gold is said to lie. The intention was to pump it dry at low tide and to dig the coins out of the sand, but a storm blew up and wrecked the dam before the water could be pumped out. In 1847 a group of Cornish tin miners dug a shaft beneath the rocks and sand in the hope of reaching the gold. They were almost drowned before they gave up.

The same shaft was used once more in 1877 in an attempt to suck the treasure out with the aid of a large pump. When this scheme failed dynamite was thrown into the shaft in the hope of blowing the coins from beneath the sand. Nothing was found following the explosion, but the next day a visitor picked up several gold coins on the shore. Since then odd coins have been found by hundreds of people and the spot has become known as Dollar Cove.

In the winter of 1807 the frigate *Anson* was blown ashore between Gunwalloe and Porthleven. At the time she was serving as a pay ship for the Channel fleet and her cargo included navy pay now valued at more than £1,000,000. Cannon thought to come from the *Anson* have been found by divers, but to this day the treasure has not been recovered. Hundreds of amateur treasure hunters equipped with detectors have visited the area during the past four years and excellent finds have been made.

The troopship *James and Rebecca* was also lost off Gunwalloe in 1807. Twenty-eight dragoons from this ship were drowned when they tried to swim ashore weighed down with gold plate. There is an even richer wreck lying on the seabed somewhere in this area. In the sixteenth-century a Portuguese privateer, the *Donna Maria*, went down with a cargo of £30,000,000 in gold.

Mount's Bay area: In November 1865, a southerly gale claimed five ships between Eastern Green and Cudden Point. On one night in 1867 four large schooners and a 500-ton barque were lost within a few hundred yards of the Mount. From 1869 to 1896 more than forty large vessels were wrecked on the four miles of coast between Porthleven and Penzance.

Land's End to St Ives: Savage storms and deadly rocks have claimed hundreds of victims on this coast. In 1659 a Dutch West Indiaman with a cargo including silver ingots was wrecked in Whitesand Bay. In 1703 the man-of-war *Colchester* also went down in the bay with a loss of one

hundred lives. More than thirty ships have been wrecked around Pendeen Watch and many more on the Carracks reef.

St Ives Bay: Another ships' graveyard. A Spanish treasure ship was lost in 1514 and eight more large ships followed her in 1516. During one night of gales in 1752 thirteen vessels sank in the bay, and more than twenty were lost in the winter of 1807.

Fig. 19 Typical rocky headland in Cornwall, a great danger to shipping in the days of sail.

Portreath area: In 1751 a Spanish ship carrying silver coins was wrecked off Portreath. In 1763 the brig *Hanover* sank in Hanover Cove. She carried £60,000 in gold coins and although official records state that the cargo was salvaged numerous gold coins were found on the beach in later years. Another brig, *Dauntless*, carrying gold dust from Africa, was driven ashore near Cligga Head in 1871.

Padstow Bay: At least 300 ships have been wrecked here during the past 150 years. Five sank in one night of storms in 1801. There is a local tradition that pirate's treasure buried by Captain John Piers lies somewhere near Harlyn Bay.

North of Padstow: During a storm in 1752 fifteen ships sank between Mouls and Tintagel.

Bude area: The earliest records report the sinking of a ship bound for Barbados in 1674. Since then hundreds have joined her on the sea bed in this area.

Tin, lead, copper, gold and silver have all been mined in Cornwall and the sites of old workings provide rich gem-collecting locations for rockhounds visiting the county. The Sennan Cove area near Land's End is one of the best in the country for amethyst which can be found on the beach and in spoil heaps near most mine shafts between Sennan and St Just. Further north between Tregeseal and Gurnard's Head beryl, tourmaline, fluorite, garnet, chalcedony, haematite and malachite can be found. To the south, beaches between St Levain and Penzance are noted for topaz, amethyst and rose quartz.

Much copper mining was formerly carred out in the district between St Ives and Camborne and derelict mines in the area are noted for specimens of green and purple flourite. Topaz, tourmaline and apatite can also be found. The Lizard peninsula consists of a great mass of serpentine which is used locally as an ornamental stone. Attractive pebbles of serpentine can be picked up on the beaches hereabouts, as can beautiful agates on beaches between The Lizard and Falmouth.

More gem-collecting locations are situated around St

Fig. 20   A Cornish holiday beach. Good for modern coins and jewellery.

Austell where fluorite, topaz, apatite, beryl, tourmaline and amethyst are found in quarries in the district. At most of the old mines between St Austell and Bodmin excellent fluorite specimens can be found. Some of the best specimens have come from the Lostwithiel and Lanlivery areas. Rocky outcrops and stream beds on Bodmin Moor can also be profitably explored for gem minerals. South of the moor good quartz crystals are found at mines near Liskeard. In the Callington area fluorite, chalcedony, and large specimens of galena have been collected, while the Launceston area east of Bodmin Moor has fluorite and serpentine.

Beaches on the north coast of Cornwall are less productive but agate pebbles can be picked up near most of the popular holiday resorts. Tintagel is noted for fine specimens of rock crystal.

As in Devon, the best prospects for bottle collecting in Cornwall are to be found in the county's numerous mining villages where undiscovered nineteenth-century dumps must contain many excellent specimens. British Bottle Collectors Club members in the county have excavated sites near Truro and Falmouth; worthwhile finds have also been made along the Camel riverside between Padstow and Wade-bridge.

Lundy Island For many centuries Lundy was a haven for pirates who attacked shipping in the Bristol Channel. In the thirteenth-century the island was held for the English Crown by Sir William de Marisco who built a castle here and spent much of his life as a part-time pirate. In the seventeenth-century a notorious pirate named Captain Salkeid declared himself King of Lundy and captured many ships before he and his crew were driven away by the English navy. A French privateer made Lundy his headquarters in the eighteenth century. After disposing of the English garrison he threw the guns from Marisco Castle and those from a smaller fort built during the Civil War into the sea. Some of these cannon were recovered in the nineteenth century, but several remain buried in the foreshore beneath Marisco Castle. Needless to say, there are many stories of pirate treasure buried on Lundy. Caves on the eastern side of the island are said to hold hidden gold, and Rat Island, which is cut off from Lundy only at high tide, is also said to be rich in pirate treasure.

Of the many wrecks which have occurred on Lundy's rocky shores at least one carried a rich cargo. This was the *Jenny*, a merchantman returning to England from Africa in the eighteenth-century with a cargo of ivory and gold dust. The point where she struck the shore is now known as Jenny's Cove and some ivory was recovered here about a hundred years ago. Caves in the area are said to contain rusted ship's fittings.

Rockhounds who visit Lundy will find excellent specimens of topaz, rock crystal and tourmaline in the many quarries on the island which are reminders of the days when Lundy was used as a convict settlement. A profitable vein of copper was found in the nineteenth century, but because of high transport costs little ore was mined.

Somerset

In the late nineteenth century large amounts of refuse from Bristol and Weston-super-Mare were taken by barge to low-lying marshes between Avonmouth and Bridgwater Bay. Four rivers in this region—the Yeo, Axe, Brue and Parrett—were in those days navigable for considerable distances and refuse barges used them to reach dumping grounds several miles from the coast. On the Yeo they travelled as far as Congresbury where much refuse from Bristol was dumped; in the south the banks of the Parrett had mooring points for barges carrying refuse from Weston and from Bridgwater. Several of these sites have been located and explored by members of the British Bottle Collectors Club who have made excellent finds of bottles, pipes and pot lids. Dumps in quarries and alongside disused canals around Bath have also produced good finds (including many coloured pot lids) during group digs organized by the club.

The best coinshooting sites in the county are also found between Bristol and Bridgwater. Many eighteenth- and nineteenth-century coins and relics have been found on the foreshores of the Avon and large numbers of Roman coins have turned up near Avonmouth Docks. The area around the Clifton Suspension Bridge has also produced many coins, while Portishead, at the mouth of the river, is noted for coins and clay tobacco pipes found on local foreshores. Half a mile upstream from the mouth of the Avon on the southern shore of the Severn is an area known as Gravel Banks where coinshooters have located Elizabethan coinage, and at Clevedon, seven miles downstream, numerous finds from the seventeenth to the nineteenth century have been made near Ladye Point. Weston-super-Mare's beaches are excellent sites for those seeking modern coins and jewellery, and the area around Steart Dykes at the mouth of the Parrett is rich in Roman coins.

Bath is undoubtedly the most likely place to produce Roman coins. Approximately 80,000 have been found in the city so far, including at least sixty hoards. Many of these finds were made in private gardens and on allotments where detector searches are certain to reveal many more. A number of hoards have also been found at other places in the county, especially near the coast where hoard locations include Portbury, Clapton, Walton, Nailsea, Wraxhall, Chelvey and Long Ashton.

Rockhounds have a good choice of sites in Somerset. There are disused lead mines in the Bridgwater district where good specimens of malachite and azurite can be found; at many of the quarries in the Mendips fluorite crystals and some rose quartz are obtainable. The beaches of Bridgwater Bay can be profitably searched for agate, quartzite and chalcedony.

4 Wales

Before railways came to south Wales in the 1850s most coal produced in the region was carried to the coast along an intricate network of canals. By 1860 almost all of this trade had been lost to railway companies, but many barge owners were able to continue in business thanks to the need for refuse disposal services in the rapidly expanding towns which grew around the ports and industrial sites on the coast. From then until the 1920s canals played an important role in the refuse disposal cycle; first as routes along which refuse was carried to quarries and clay pits, and finally as sites where refuse could be dumped when the quarries and pits had been filled.

Newport on the River Usk was the terminal point of the Monmouthshire Canal which was constructed in the late eighteenth and early nineteenth centuries. It ran from Newport to Pontypool via Cwmbran, with a branch from Crindai to Crumlin, and it could accommodate barges sixty-four feet long by nine feet wide. In 1880 the canal was sold to the Great Western Railway Company and the Newport section was filled in to make a railway line. Today its weed-choked banks around Newport, Cwmbran, Pontypool and Crumlin provide Monmouthshire dump diggers with excellent bottle-hunting sites.

The Glamorganshire Canal linked Cardiff with Merthyr Tydfil and provided cheap transport for iron ore, coal and limestone from 1794 until 1890 when railway competition put the canal company out of business. A plan to fill in the section between Cardiff and Trefforest for use as a railway line was put forward in 1897 but the line subsequently built did not use the canal bed. Nevertheless, the canal was soon derelict and without water for part of its length following a burst. The section around Merthyr Tydfil was filled in before the end of the nineteenth century and in Cardiff much of it was built over. Several excellent bottle dumps have been located along its banks by British Bottle Collectors Club members.

The Neath Canal continued to attract traffic up to 1934

South Wales

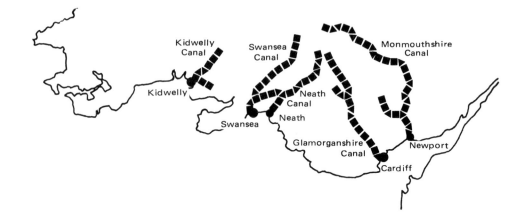

Fig. 21 Canals of south Wales. There are many Victorian refuse sites along their banks.

and it still finds a use today as a source of water. It was opened in 1791 and ran from Briton Ferry to Glyneath. Refuse barges used it to reach dumps along its banks between Neath and Ynysygerwyn in the late nineteenth century and it was one of these sites which was discovered in a rather unusual way in 1973 when a fisherman from Neath was searching for worms near Aberdulais. Using only a penknife, he dug from the banks three rare Codd-Hamilton hybrids and several transfer ginger beers. Fortunately he mentioned these finds to a friend who is a member of the British Bottle Collectors Club and since then several group digs have been organized on the site. Excellent dumps have also been located on the banks of the Swansea Canal between Swansea and Clydach. Research suggests that others await discovery along the upper reaches of the canal between Ystalyfera and Hen Neuadd where much of the channel has been filled in. West of Swansea there are derelict canals around Pen-Clawdd, Pembrey and Kidwelly which have yet to be thoroughly explored by dump diggers.

Some of the most interesting coins and relics found by amateur treasure hunters in south Wales have come from the foreshores of the Severn Estuary. Roman coins have been found around Beachley Point at the mouth of the River Wye and medieval coins and tokens are included in the relics recovered further upstream at Chepstow. Newport on the Usk is an ancient port with a tidal foreshore rich in eighteenth- and nineteenth-century coins and clay tobacco pipes. The areas beneath the town's bridges are

62

especially productive. The river has also proved rich in Roman relics in its upper reaches around Caerleon, once a Roman legionary fortress.

The site of another Roman town at Caerwent near Newport has produced excellent finds of Roman and medieval coins. In 1917 a farmer digging his potato field near the east wall of the old town found several early Saxon silver coins; eight years later a number of silver groats of Henry VIII were discovered on the same spot. At least five Roman hoards have also been found within three miles of this site.

Cardiff has some excellent coinshooting locations including Cathay's Park, Roath Park and Bute Park where Victorian coins and jewellery have turned up. In the dockland areas of the River Taff clay tobacco pipes, tokens, and a

Fig. 22 A derelict canal in south Wales.

rich assortment of coins, medals and badges have been found. Especially good finds have been made in the Grangetown and Penarth Flats areas. Readers seeking large amounts of modern coinage will find the beaches of nearby Barry Island highly productive. Porthcawl's sandy beaches are also noted for their modern coins, but the village of Newton, now part of Porthcawl, was the scene of an exciting treasure hunt in 1930 when schoolchildren playing in the ruins of a derelict public house in the village found several antique coins and an old leather wallet hidden behind a loose brick in the fireplace. When opened, the wallet was found to contain a plan of the public house on which were written directions to indicate the whereabouts of a hoard of gold coins. Every able-bodied man, woman and child in the village was digging frantically on the site within an hour and more than twenty tons of stone were moved in an effort to find a flight of stairs leading to a cellar beneath the foundations where the gold was said to be hidden. One man found a single bronze coin in the rubble, but the stairs were not located. Frustrated by their lack of success the villagers declared the story a hoax and returned to their homes. The cellar and the gold—if they ever existed—remain undiscovered.

On the other side of Swansea Bay, seventeenth- and eighteenth-century coins and at least one ship's cannon have been found around Mumbles Head where many shipwrecks have occurred. Cliffs in the neighbourhood are said to have been used by smugglers and there is a local tradition that treasure is buried within the vicinity of Oystermouth Castle. At the opposite end of the Gower Peninsula the beach between Worms Head and Rhossili is probably the best location in Wales on which to hunt for shipwreck treasure. At low tide the skeleton of the *Helvetia*, wrecked in 1887, can be seen buried in the sand here, and many Victorian coins including gold sovereigns have been found near the wreck by beachcombers. A Spanish ship carrying a rich cargo of silver coins was also wrecked on this beach in the seventeenth century. In 1807 a severe storm washed up thousands of silver coins and Rhossili Bay was the scene of a

Fig. 23 Bottles from a dump in south Wales.

wild silver rush as local farmers and fishermen staked claims along the foreshore and picked up a small fortune while the storm raged. In 1883 high tides and rough seas produced a second crop of coins, most of which were found by a man named Lucas who fled the country with his fortune. Since then a steady supply of coins have come ashore and many have been found in recent years by detector users.

Readers who enjoy the excitement of river raking will find much to interest them on the foreshores of the River Towy between Kidwelly and Carmarthen. The riverbanks exposed at low tide have produced fifteenth- and sixteenth-century coins and several weapons including swords and spearheads. Tenby Castle on the western side of Carmarthen Bay has also produced many weapons; they have come from the beach below Castle Hill and from the local harbour where eighteenth- and nineteenth-century coins also turn up. The castle at Pembroke is surrounded on three sides by tidal water and it is from the muddy foreshores hereabouts that many Civil War relics including cannonballs, swords and coins have been recovered. Several coin hoards have also been found within the town. Milford Haven and Fishguard also have tidal foreshores which produce good finds, while the site beneath the ancient bridge in Cardigan is highly productive of seventeenth- and eighteenth-century relics.

The Pembrokeshire and Cardiganshire coasts have excellent shingle beaches where a variety of colourful pebbles including agate, quartzite and chalcedony can be picked up. Inland there are quarries between Haverford-west and Fishguard where specimens of diorite and apatite can be found, and on Strumble Head where jasper, quartz and haematite occur. In Carmarthenshire amethyst and smoky quartz are to be found near disused mines around Llandovery; in Glamorganshire jasper, agate and potato stones can be found at Llantrisant north-west of Cardiff.

North Wales Rockhounds hoping to find nuggets of gold should try their luck around Dolgellau in Merionethshire where gold has been mined on local mountainsides since Roman times. It has also been obtained by panning in local streams. In the same county are many abandoned copper and lead mines where excellent specimens of malachite, azurite and rock crystal may be obtained. The best locations lie around the town of Ffestiniog. In Denbighshire the mines near Betws-y-Coed and Llanrwst are noted for clear quartz crystals and epidote. In neighbouring Flintshire the area around Halkyn Mountain is dotted with derelict zinc and lead mines where excellent purple fluorite can be found. On the coast, beaches near Prestatyn have cornelian, agate and quartzite pebbles.

Caernarvonshire's minerals include malachite and azurite to be found on Great Ormes Head near Llandudno. Beaches in the area have pebbles of jasper, chalcedony and agate. There are derelict copper mines on the Lleyn Peninsula where malachite and serpentine can be found, and in Snowdonia where gold has occasionally been found in quartz veins. In the Pass of Llanberis many of the veins

66

Fig. 24 Rare Victorian
bottles from another
south Wales dump.

carry pale green quartz and epidote. Across the Menai
Straits Anglesey's quarries and overgrown spoil heaps are
worth exploring for serpentine, malachite and agate.

Most experienced detector users who visit north Wales
try their luck on Anglesey's shores in the hope of locating
wreck treasure. The best finds have undoubtedly come from
Moelfre beach where the *Royal Charter* was driven ashore by
a hurricane in 1859. One of the finest vessels in the Liverpool and Australian Navigation Company's fleet, she was an
iron, full-rigged sailing ship fitted with a 200 h.p. auxiliary
engine and she was homeward bound from Melbourne when

disaster struck. Most of her passengers were gold diggers returning to Britain after years of work in Australia's goldfields; between them they carried more than half a million pounds worth of gold. There was another half million pounds in coined and uncoined gold bullion in her cargo and when a great wave blown up by the hurricane broke the ship in two and threw the wreckage onto Moelfre beach the bulk of her treasure was spilled onto the sand between high and low water marks.

Even before the bodies of the four hundred and fifty-nine passengers and crew who perished had been buried people in the district were scooping gold sovereigns by the hundred from rocky pools and shingle patches in the neighbourhood. Customs officials who arrived on the scene a few days later put a stop to this enterprise and collected many of the coins that had been found. When added to the gold recovered in later salvage operations the total reached £300,000. The unrecovered coins and raw gold were soon buried deep in the sand and it is this stockpile—now worth several million pounds—that continues to supply the beach with occasional sovereigns after stormy weather. I was recently shown six gold coins found on the beach in 1973 and I was amazed by their near perfect condition after more than a century beneath the sand. Silver coins have also been found on beaches south of Moelfre in Red Wharf Bay. They are believed to come from a Spanish treasure ship driven ashore here in the seventeenth-century.

On the opposite side of the island hundreds of shipwrecks have occurred between Rhosneigr and Rhoscolyn where local beaches have produced numerous coins. In the eighteenth century this coast was plagued by wreckers who lured many ships to destruction. A particularly notorious band of wreckers known as the Crigyll Robbers used to hide their fortune in sand dunes near Rhosneigr until they were caught and imprisoned at Beaumaris in 1715. Other Anglesey beaches on which wreck coinage can be found include Church Bay, Cemaes Bay, and Dulas Bay. There are also several excellent coinshooting sites along the shores of the Menai Straits. At Caernarvon coins of all periods are

68

Fig. 25 Ginger beers from north Wales.

found in the river beneath the castle walls. At Bangor and Beaumaris many Victorian coins have been recovered near the old Menai Ferry sites and in Beaumaris harbour; the foreshores beneath Menai Bridge are also rich in nineteenth-century coins.

On the north coast of Wales there are many miles of golden sands and several popular resorts including Prestatyn, Rhyl, Colwyn Bay and Llandudno where scores of thousands of modern coins have been lost by holidaymakers. At Prestatyn the most productive sites are Central, Ffrith and Barkley beaches, while the beach near the pier at Rhyl is the best site for those who wish to find the largest possible number of coins in a short time. Fewer but much older finds can be made around Rhuddlan Castle some three miles from

69

Rhyl where sixteenth- and seventeenth-century coins have recently been located. Colwyn Bay's main beach is rich in modern coins, but the best Victorian specimens have been found in woods around the town. Near Llandudno a hoard of 500 Roman coins and several gold ornaments was found in 1907 on Little Ormes Head. They were in an earthenware jar buried at the foot of the limestone precipice which forms the southern face of the headland. Roman coins have also been found on nearby Great Ormes Head in recent years.

During the summer of 1972 the British Amateur Treasure Hunting Club held one of its regular outings on the tidal foreshores of the River Conway near the ancient castle. Twenty-five members equipped with detectors took part in the search and a total of 220 coins was found in one afternoon. They included two Elizabethan specimens, several of Charles I, and a large number of Victorian pennies and shillings. Two cannonballs and a brass ring were also found. The river undoubtedly holds much more—including freshwater pearls which can be found further upstream above Llantwst.

The Lleyn Peninsula in Caernarvonshire is another area rich in amateur treasure hunting locations. At Dinas Dinlle a Spanish ship carrying much treasure was driven ashore in the eighteenth century. Large numbers of coins turned up on the beach during the months following the disaster and one local man who picked up enough to fill a sack was almost drowned because of their weight when the tide came in rather sooner than he expected. They continue to wash up onto the beach to this day, though not in such great numbers. There was much smuggling along this coast in the eighteenth century and the main centre was at Porth Dinllaen. According to local tradition contraband was hidden in the roofs of houses in the village and on Bardsey Island off the tip of the peninsula. Here monastic treasure has been found in the past and more is reputed to await discovery. Aberdaron on the mainland was once the main port of embarkation for thousands of pilgrims who visited holy shrines on Bardsey in medieval times.

On the other side of the peninsula Pwllheli's beaches are

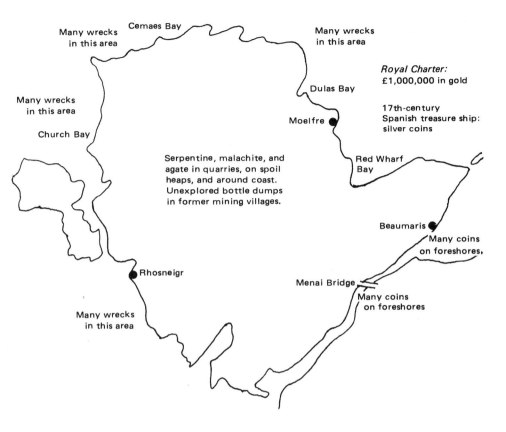

Many wrecks
in this area

Cemaes Bay

Many wrecks
in this area

Royal Charter:
£1,000,000 in gold

Dulas Bay

Many wrecks
in this area

Church Bay

Moelfre

17th-century
Spanish treasure ship:
silver coins

Serpentine, malachite, and
agate in quarries, on spoil
heaps, and around coast.
Unexplored bottle dumps
in former mining villages.

Red Wharf
Bay

Beaumaris

Many coins
on foreshores,

Rhosneigr

Menai Bridge

Many coins
on foreshores

Many wrecks
in this area

rich in modern coins and the harbour is noted for Victorian
relics including clay tobacco pipes and silver coinage.
Further along the coast there is a ruined castle at Criccieth
which stands on a rock in the centre of the shore. Around it
medieval finds have recently been made and several weapons
recovered. Barmouth on the Merionethshire coast made
news in the 1920s when a contractor inspecting the damaged
seawalls on the foreshore found a number of antique coins
embedded in the foundations. They were all of different
dates and did not appear to come from a wreck. More
recently a number of eighteenth-century finds were made
in 1970 by amateur treasure hunters who searched the tidal
foreshores of the River Mawdock beneath the town's
bridge.

Fig. 26 Anglesey—for
treasure hunters.

Fig. 27 Coins from riversides in north Wales.

Most bottle collectors in north Wales have concentrated on finding small dumps near former mining villages in the mountainous regions or on searching the foreshores of the Dee estuary in Flintshire where some of Chester's refuse was dumped in the late nineteenth century. Research suggests that more profitable sites might be found along the disused Shropshire Union Canal between Newtown in Montgomeryshire and the Shropshire border. The Llangollen Canal in Denbighshire is still in use, but Victorian dumps probably await discovery along its banks.

5 Northern England

Most detector users who visit Lancashire during their holidays make for Blackpool, Southport, or Morecambe where the beaches are unsurpassed as coinshooting sites. Since 1972 a group of Lancashire amateur treasure hunters have regularly worked Blackpool's golden sands during the summer months and their finds have averaged one hundred and fifty coins per man after every tide. The coins recovered are, of course, almost all modern, but after rough weather a few Edwardian and late Victorian specimens are brought up from deep beneath the sand. Readers prepared to face the savage winter winds experienced on this coast will find the proportion of early coins turned up here increase dramatically between November and March when heavy seas plough the sand to a depth of two feet or more.

At many places along Lancashire's coastline the sea has been retreating for hundreds of years and the sand left behind has been piled into dunes by the prevailing winds. As a result several former fishing villages and ports are now high and dry—cut off from the sea by ridges of sand. In 1911 a severe gale moved one of these sand ridges near the village of Ainsdale, north of Blackpool, a distance of one hundred yards. In so doing it exposed the wrecks of seven wooden ships of between two and three hundred tons. They lay in a neat row, one against the other, and it was assumed a river had at one time entered the sea hereabouts and that the vessels had been beached at its mouth. They remained visible for several days until a second gale buried them beneath the sand once more. At Formby, now two miles from the sea, the old harbour and several houses have also disappeared under the dunes.

Lytham, at the mouth of the River Ribble, was one of the first seaside resorts on the Lancashire coast. It attracted visitors as early as 1812 and was the county's premier resort by 1870. Today much of its holiday trade has been lost to Blackpool, but Lytham's foreshores still repay attention because they hold substantial amounts of Victorian coinage It was at Lytham that a corporation gardener working in a

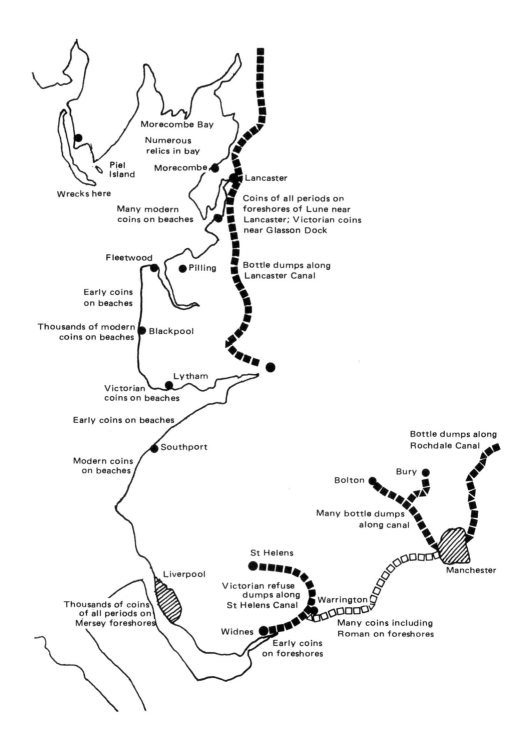

Morecombe Bay
Numerous
relics in bay

Piel
Island

Morecombe

Lancaster

Wrecks here

Coins of all periods on
foreshores of Lune near
Lancaster; Victorian coins
near Glasson Dock

Many modern
coins on beaches

Fleetwood

Pilling

Bottle dumps along
Lancaster Canal

Early coins
on beaches

Thousands of modern
coins on beaches

Blackpool

Lytham

Victorian
coins on beaches

Early coins on beaches

Southport

Modern coins
on beaches

Bottle dumps along
Rochdale Canal

Bury

Bolton

Many bottle dumps
along canal

St Helens

Manchester

Liverpool

Victorian refuse
dumps along
St Helens Canal

Warrington

Thousands of coins
of all periods on
Mersey foreshores

Widnes

Many coins including
Roman on foreshores

Early coins
on foreshores

local park dug up a valuable hoard in 1961. The pot he found contained 381 gold and silver coins dated 1550–1600.

At Blackpool the most likely place to find Victorian coins is on the beach beneath North Pier which was built in 1862, but much earlier coinage has been found after severe storms on the coast north of the town. Several villages, inns and churches are said to have been lost to the

Fig. 28 (*facing*) Lancashire for coinshooters and dump diggers.

Fig. 29 (*above*) Blackpool Beach, where a fortune in modern coins and jewellery lies beneath the golden sands.

Fig. 30 Bottles from Lancashire dumps.

sea in this area; in the 1880s remains of houses and a number of coins were found on the beach during a particularly low tide at Norbreck.

The sea has also caused considerable damage to the coastline between Fleetwood and Lancaster in the past. At Pilling forty houses were swept away in 1720 and at Cockersand much of the abbey has been lost. There have also been numerous shipwrecks on the treacherous sandbanks hereabouts; in the seventeenth century villagers in Pilling augmented their incomes by patrolling the shores to find wreckage cast up by the tides. More recently excellent finds have been made by detector users between Knott End and Braides. At Knott End in 1926 a hoard of 400 Roman coins was found when sand was dug from the golf course. After workmen had removed the hoard, hens scratching in the sand revealed over one hundred more coins. A similar find was made nearby at Rossall in 1840.

Fig. 31 Bottles from
dumps near
Manchester.

Further north the quicksands of Morecambe Bay have
claimed many lives and much property. In the fifteenth
century, official guides were appointed to take travellers
across the bay at low tide on a route from Ulveston to Hest
Bank via Flookburgh and Grange-over-Sands. These guides

77

THIS DENTIFRICE
IS COMPOUNDED ACCORDING
TO THE PRESCRIPTION OF
C.R.COFFIN.D.D.S.
(BALTIMORE COLLEGE OF DENTAL SURGERY)
PREPARED ONLY BY
WILLIAM DARLING
Chemist
126. OXFORD STREET MANCHESTER.
AMERICAN DENTIFRICE

Fig. 32 Pot lid from a dump near Manchester.

were recruited from local cockle-fishing families who knew the safe passages, but there were many disasters because the quicksands were constantly moving. In the eighteenth and early nineteenth centuries there was a regular coach service across the sands which suffered heavy losses when horses and coaches sank into quicksand. On 3 March, 1817 the *Whitehaven Belle*, carrying eight passengers and several bags of mail, was trapped on the Leven sands when a gust of wind overturned the coach. The driver managed to cut two of the horses free and he used them to take passengers to Bolton-le-Sands. Next day the coach was found with two drowned horses still in its shafts, but it was so firmly embedded in the sand salvage proved impossible. Similar accidents continued until the railway line from Carnforth to Barrow-in-Furness was opened in the late nineteenth century.

There can be no doubt that many exciting finds await the determined treasure hunter in Morecambe Bay, but readers are warned that even today the sands are dangerous to those who do not know their moods. Mists can come down with

terrifying suddenness and the tides often behave in unpredic-
table ways. It is of the utmost importance that visitors do not
stray far from recognized routes and that crossings are timed
to give a good margin of safety. It is not necessary to
venture far into the bay to find good sites: excellent coins
have been recovered near Carnforth in recent years and there
are many wrecks on the other side of the bay around Piel
Island where seventeenth- and eighteenth-century relics can
be found.

Lancashire's industrial rivers are somewhat neglected by
amateur treasure hunters, which is a pity because they hold a
rich assortment of eighteenth- and nineteenth-century coins
and some have much earlier treasures along their banks.

Fig. 34 Found in a derelict house in Lancashire.

The Mersey estuary is richest of all and in many places compares favourably with the Thames as a source of collectable relics. Near Liverpool the industrial debris littering the foreshores at Seaforth, Aighurth and Speke can be sieved to locate coins, tokens, seals, clay tobacco pipes, and many military buttons and badges. Similar finds can be made at Widnes and Warrington where Roman coins also litter the riverbed.

At Preston on the River Ribble a number of Civil War coins have been found on the foreshore in recent years together with many eighteenth- and nineteenth-century coins. Two miles above Preston at Cuerdale the largest hoard of tenth-century coins ever found in Britain was discovered on the banks of the river in 1840. Workmen repairing a wall near the ancient ford at Cuerdale uncovered a lead chest buried a few yards from the crossing; when opened it was found to contain 10,000 English and Northumbrian coins and 1,000 ounces of silver ingots. Numismatists who examined the coins were able to say that the hoard had probably been buried in 911 by a Danish army overtaken in its retreat from Northumbria. At another site on the Ribble, where it is joined by the River Calder, workmen laying pipes in the adjacent meadow dug up a hoard of Celtic gold jewellery in 1966.

Lancaster on the River Lune is another ancient port with foreshores which hold numerous relics of the city's long history. The castle which dominates it changed hands twice during the Civil War and was occupied by the Jacobites in 1715 and 1745. Coins of these periods have been found in the river, as have many eighteenth-century relics near St George's Quay where sailing ships returning from the West Indies unloaded their cargoes of sugar, rum, tobacco and cotton. Remains of the old quays can still be seen on the riverside and it is from around them that the best finds have come. When the river began to silt up in the late eighteenth century, new wharves were built further downstream at Glasson Dock where many Victorian coins can be found today.

Since 1176 the county assizes have been held in Lancaster

and until the end of the seventeenth century condemned prisoners were taken by open cart from the castle prison to the moor on the outskirts of the town where they were publicly hanged. The executions attracted large crowds and provided an excuse for a day of merrymaking which must have caused many coins to be lost on the moor. It was on Halton Moor five miles from Lancaster that a valuable hoard was discovered in the nineteenth century when a

Fig. 35 A derelict canal in Lancashire.

81

Fig. 36 Finds from the River Mersey.

farmer dug up a silver cup containing 850 coins of King Canute.

Bottle collectors who visit Lancashire will find numerous Victorian refuse sites along the banks of the county's disused canals. The St Helens Canal is derelict for its entire length from St Helens to Widnes, as is the Manchester, Bolton and Bury Canal. Both have dumps along their banks which hold a rich assortment of bottles, pipes and pot lids from Liverpool, Manchester, and several other towns. Much of Victorian Manchester's refuse was also dumped along the banks of the partly derelict Rochdale Canal on the outskirts of Manchester. In the north of the county the Lancaster Canal was used as a refuse disposal route for much of that city's nineteenth-century refuse.

Yorkshire   No other county in Britain can offer holiday treasure hunters so varied a selection of bottle collecting, rockhounding, and coinshooting sites as are available in Yorkshire. It has one of the most active branches of the British Bottle Collectors Club and there are three highly successful

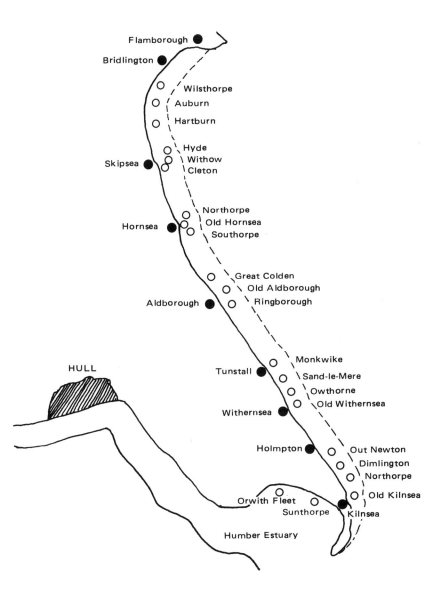

Flamborough
Bridlington
Wilsthorpe
Auburn
Hartburn
Hyde
Withow
Cleton
Skipsea
Northorpe
Old Hornsea
Hornsea
Southorpe
Great Colden
Old Aldborough
Aldborough
Ringborough
HULL
Monkwike
Tunstall
Sand-le-Mere
Owthorne
Old Withernsea
Withernsea
Holmpton
Out Newton
Dimlington
Northorpe
Orwith Fleet
Old Kilnsea
Sunthorpe
Kilnsea
Humber Estuary

Fig. 37 Lost villages on
the Yorkshire coast.
The dotted line shows
the Roman coastline.

treasure hunters' clubs within its borders. Add to this the
rich selection of rockhounding sites in its former lead
mining regions and along its delightful coastline and the
reason why there are so many successful Yorkshire enthusiasts becomes obvious.

The best-known and most productive Victorian refuse

83

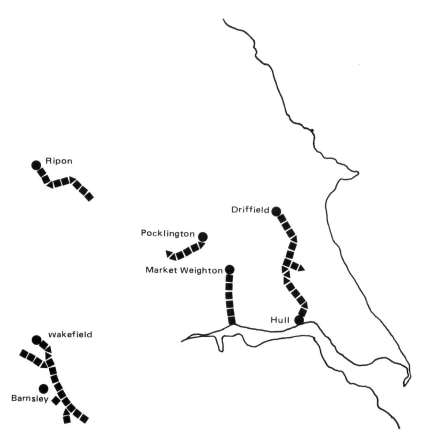

Fig. 38 Derelict canals in Yorkshire.

sites yet discovered in Yorkshire are those around Harrogate where digging commenced in the early months of 1974. The number of pot lids so far recovered on these dumps is fast approaching that of first-class sites around London, and the rare bottles that have been dug up include Warner's 'Safe' Cures, Radam's Microbe Killers, brown Codd's, Ryland's Valves, and Barrett and Elers' Wooden Plugs. The reason why this comparatively small town's nineteenth-century refuse sites have proved so rich in valuable finds is that Harrogate was an internationally famous spa which attracted millions of Victorian visitors between 1850 and 1900. The majority of these visitors were rich and they ate well, drank well, and could afford to buy expensive quack medicines—hence the quality of the refuse they threw away.

84

Fig. 39 Finds from the foreshores of the River Ouse in Yorkshire.

Scarborough on the coast was an equally famous Victorian watering place and its dumps, which have yet to be found, are certain to hold similar finds. Research suggests that refuse was once thrown into pits on the outskirts of the town along the railway line to York. In York the bulk of nineteenth-century refuse was carted to low-lying marshes near Foss Island or taken by barge down the Ouse below Naburn Lock where it was discharged into the river. I recently talked to an old fisherman who as a boy had helped his father net salmon on the Ouse between Naburn and Cawood. He recalled that old bottles lying on the bed of the river were a considerable nuisance because they were forever fouling the nets. He admitted to breaking hundreds of Codd's and Hamilton's hauled out of the river but felt certain thousands more had escaped his nets and his anger.

Elsewhere in the county the banks of derelict canals are rich in dumps. At Driffield part of the local canal has been filled in with refuse and there are dumps containing rubbish from both Driffield and Hull along the banks of the River Hull between the two towns. Higher on the Humber estuary the Market Weighton Canal has been largely filled in as has the Pocklington Canal to the north. In the West Riding there are several unexplored and much overgrown

85

Fig. 40 Yorkshire
Dales rockhounding
sites.

canals around Barnsley where, as every bottle collector
knows, most Codd's bottles were manufactured. No one
has yet found the sites where unwanted bottles produced by
Rylands' Glass Works in Barnsley were dumped but it is
certain that the fortunate collector who does locate one of
these sites will uncover a vast hoard of Codd's, Rylands'
Valves, and other prize specimens. The sites probably lie
somewhere along those derelict canals. Several canalside
dumps around Halifax, Bradford and Leeds have been

86

located by British Bottle Collectors Club members and group digs are held regularly on most of them.

Nowadays the Yorkshire Dales attract thousands of tourists on every holiday weekend, but in the nineteenth century this part of Yorkshire was known only to sheep farmers and lead miners. The latter left numerous derelict mining sites when the rich ores became exhausted at the beginning of this century and it is the spoil heaps around them which interest present-day rockhounds. They are rich in semi-precious crystals of fluorite and other attractive specimens and they have been visited by fewer collectors than have better known sites in Devon and Cornwall.

Fig. 41 Ginger beers from a Yorkshire dump.

Consequently it is much easier to find large specimens. The following locations are worth visiting and are certain to provide the diligent rockhound with good finds:

Malham Moor: North-west of Malham village there are spoil heaps containing galena, malachite, quartz and calcite. Between Grizedale and Kirby Fell there are unworked veins containing malachite, quartz and iron pyrites.

Grassington Moor: On the Low Moor spoil heaps around disused mines contain fluorite and calcite; on the High Moor finds of fluorite, calcite, malachite and quartz crystals have been made.

Coniston Moor: Spoil heaps and unworked veins carry galena, fluorite, calcite and zinc blende.

Kettlewell: On the slopes of Great Whernside there are numerous old lead workings where galena, pyrites, fluorite and calcite can be found.

Buckden: On Buckden Moor and Starbotton Fell calcite and fluorite are obtained.

Greenhow: On the moors around Greenhow village fluorite and calcite can be found near old workings. The fluorite occurs in yellow, green, mauve and deep purple varieties; the calcite crystals are occasionally pink or dark brown.

Appletreewick: There are many old lead mines in this area and until recently opencast mining for fluorite was carried on. Spoil heaps and abandoned quarries are rich in fluorite specimens.

The Yorkshire coast from Saltburn to Withernsea has many shingle beaches where jasper, agate, quartz and chalcedony can be found. In the Whitby area water-worn pieces of jet can be picked up on the beach, but the largest and most valuable jet specimens are to be found in cliff faces north and south of Whitby or at inland sites where it was mined in the nineteenth century. The shales which carry jet seams should be sought in the cliffs at Robin Hood's Bay, Whitby, Sandsend, Kettleness, Runswick Bay, Port

Mulgrave, and Boulby where jet is always accompanied by numerous fossils. Old workings can also be found on inland valley slopes in Eskdale, Danby Dale and Kildale. If searches are carried out in Eskdale readers should also try their luck at finding freshwater pearls in the River Esk. Pearl mussels can be obtained from the river and its tributaries between Sleights and Egton Bridge.

Whitby harbour is an excellent site on which to hunt amateur treasures with a rake and sieve. On the last occasion I visited the town a single shovelful of material dug from the riverbank beneath the bridge produced three George III pennies and an equal number of lead fishing weights of uncertain vintage. Other amateur treasure hunters working in the harbour have sieved out hammered silver coins and much Victorian jewellery. Rocks in the area have claimed hundreds of small sailing ships in the past and coins from them wash up on beaches north and south of the harbour entrance where large amounts of modern coinage can also be found. Further north the beach at Redcar has produced gold sovereigns in recent years. A number were found in 1970 when heavy seas washed away loose sand on the beach and exposed the rotting timbers of several old vessels.

In the eastern part of the county the coast between Flamborough Head and Spurn Head is subject to constant erosion. The sites of more than twenty villages now lie below the high tide mark and numerous relics including tools, church bells, brass door knockers and many coins are regularly washed up from them after stormy weather. The coins are of all periods from Roman to Victorian and the largest single find so far made was at Barmston in 1933 when a fisherman walking along the foreshore found a hoard of Roman coins. Similar finds can be made in the Humber estuary between Spurn Head and Sunk Island.

At Hull some of the finest clay tobacco pipes yet recovered by amateur treasure hunters have come from the harbour where eighteenth- and nineteenth-century coins can also be found. There is a very active amateur treasure hunting group in Hull and in recent years its members have concentrated their searches on allotment gardens in and

Fig. 42 Early bottles from a Yorkshire site.

around the city. Their successes include the finding of Celtic gold coins, many silver coins from the sixteenth and seventeenth centuries, and numerous nineteenth-century relics. Further upstream at Brough-on-Humber there was a Roman settlement on the foreshore where a busy ferry carried goods and passengers across the river. Hundreds of

Roman coins have been found on these foreshores by detector users.

The banks of the River Ouse between Goole and York are rich in coinshooting sites. The foreshores at Old Goole have produced exceptionally good finds of nineteenth-century coins and tokens, and the site beneath the bridge at Selby yields coins from the past three hundred years during exceptionally low tides. At York the Ouse is no longer tidal but Roman and medieval coins and relics can be raked from the river beneath the city's bridges. The point where the River Foss joins the main river is highly productive of coins and relics from all periods. Profitable coinshooting sites around York include the racecourse and the old towpaths along the river between the city and Naburn. Elsewhere in Yorkshire parks and moors in and around Harrogate, Leeds, Ilkley and Sheffield have proved rich in lost coins and relics.

In addition to the dozens of Roman hoards found in and around the ancient city of York there have been many finds of buried treasure in other parts of the county. At Bossal, eight miles from York, a lead box containing 270 silver coins and many pieces of silver from stirrups and horse bits was dug up in a field near the Lobster House Inn in 1807. It is thought the hoard was buried by looters after the battle of Stamford Bridge in 1066. Quite a different hoard was found in Hull in 1946 when Mrs. Florence Watt of Princes Avenue decided to clean the chimney in one of her bedrooms. When she pushed the brush up the flue, out fell a biscuit tin containing £600 in old notes.

At Swine, a few miles from Hull, several hundred Roman bronze coins were dug up in 1964 in a local field within a short distance of the spot where a similar hoard was discovered in 1940. Another coincidence occurred at High Hunsley, also near Hull in 1967, when a gold bracelet ploughed up by a farmer turned out to be identical to one of four bracelets ploughed up a few miles away at Cottingham in the nineteenth century. A valuable hoard of guinea pieces dated 1725–9 was found near the Priory Church at Bridlington in 1922, but it is the story of a find of Roman silver coins at Argham near Bridlington in 1869 which intrigues many Yorkshire treasure hunters. In that year a mole catcher doing his rounds picked up several silver coins on a mole cast near the remains of a Roman site in the village. All the coins found were of a similar date and excellently preserved. It is highly probable that they came from a buried hoard but the mole catcher neither dug for more nor marked the spot on which he had found them. If a hoard did indeed lie buried beneath the soil it remains to this day.

In the North Riding a rich treasure was discovered at Egton in 1928 when workmen demolishing an old Roman Catholic Mass House in the village found a bag of silver coins dated 1562–1649 together with a handsome alms dish hidden in the thatched roof. Further north at Kirkleatham an even larger hoard of silver coins was found at Yearby Farm in 1955. The farm manager was ploughing the field opposite Kirkleatham Hall when his plough struck what appeared to be a stone. Closer examination revealed it to be a large earthenware jar which the plough had broken. Coins of Mary and Philip, Elizabeth I, James I, James II, Charles I, Charles II and William III had scattered from it and it took some time for the manager to pick up those he could see. The total came to 1,187.

I visited Yearby Farm in 1973 and talked to the present occupier about the field from which a number of other coins have been recovered since 1955. They are all of much later dates than those found in the original hoard and suggest the possibility of other hoards still buried there. According to local tradition money was buried in the field during the eighteenth and early nineteenth centuries by people seeking admission to Kirkleatham Hall, which at that time was a paupers' hospital. It has also been suggested that the first hoard contained money stolen from the hall in the seventeenth century.

In the West Riding a large hoard of Roman coins was discovered at Castleberg Quarries near Settle in 1783 and a similar find was made in Victoria Cave, also close to the town, in 1837. At Skipton an unusual find was made in 1958 when five silver coins of Edward I were discovered

Fig. 43 Bottles from a
Yorkshire dump.

hidden in the bolt hole of a door at Skipton Castle; at
Bingley a farmer cutting a drain in a field at Marton Bank
in 1775 struck a copper chest buried about twenty inches
beneath the surface which contained nearly one hundred
pounds in weight of Roman coins and a silver statue of a
goddess.

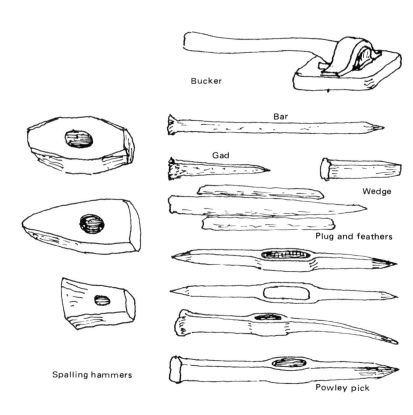

Bucker

Bar

Gad

Wedge

Plug and feathers

Spalling hammers

Powley pick

Many finds have been made around Leeds—a hoard of Roman silver on Pudsey Common in 1775 and a second of seventeenth-century coins in 1833; a leather purse containing 41 Civil War coins hidden in an old wall at Garforth; Tudor and Stuart coins at Scholes in 1924; and two earthenware jars containing a total of 300 Roman silver coins at Allerton Bywater in the same year. Treasure reputedly buried at Kirkstall Abbey in Leeds has yet to be recovered.

A spectacular garden treasure was unearthed in 1932 at Elland when a man planting potatoes in Elizabeth Street found a pot containing 1,807 silver coins dated 1520 to 1605. Less valuable but still worth finding was the jar containing £500 in banknotes dug up in a garden at Vernon Road in Harrogate in 1947. In the south a large hoard of Roman bronze coins was found in 1935 in Edlington Wood near

Doncaster, and at Bawtry on the Lincolnshire border Roman silver coins were found on the outskirts of the town in 1964. Three years earlier a single gold coin in extremely fine condition which might have come from a hoard was dug up in a garden at Highfield Road, Bawtry.

One of the most fascinating treasure stories comes from the Yorkshire Dales where a cave known locally as Boggart Hole is traditionally believed to hold hidden gold. About forty years ago flood water pouring from an underground stream washed a number of silver coins of Edward I out of the cave mouth. Most people in the district agreed the old story about hidden wealth must have been only partly true, but a few shook their heads at this idea and insisted time would prove the legend true. A few years later a second flood washed out several gold coins and restored faith in the story. Attempts have since been made to find the hidden treasure but so far they have all failed.

Durham

The wild and beautiful moors of West Durham have only recently been 'discovered' by tourists; ten years ago the region was a no-man's-land between the Lake District and the north-east coast through which most people drove their cars as fast as possible. Now all that is changing. The deserted villages of Teesdale and Weardale have been given a new lease of life by a growing army of summer visitors with money to spend on ices, postcards and souvenirs who overcrowd the streets of Barnard Castle, Middleton, Westgate, and Allenhead but who rarely stray from the main roads and their cars.

For those prepared to leave these centres and explore the heart of West Durham there are rich prizes to be found around the long-abandoned lead mines on the moorland hills where few have set foot since the ores ran out fifty or more years ago. In 1800 there were eighty-six lead mines in County Durham; by 1900 the number had dwindled to less than a dozen. Teesdale's ores were first to expire and it is on the hills above Teesdale that the oldest and most overgrown spoil heaps are found. Dig into almost any one of them between Middleton and Cross Fell and you will find excel-

95

Fig. 45 Elders growing on the site of an old dump in County Durham.

lent deep purple flourite crystals. In Weardale fluorite is still mined for use in steel-making processes and the modern spoil heaps are worth exploring for crystals which might be purple, pale blue, green, or yellow. Many of the old lead-mining sites in Weardale are also rich in rock crystal, calcite and haematite. On Alston Moor in the west there are more abandoned mines where fluorite, quartz, brown, blue, and grey chalcedony, malachite and pyrites can be found. Because few of the dumps have been explored by earlier rockhounds some hard work must be put in to clear weed growth in order to expose the material beneath. The effort is usually well rewarded.

The British Bottle Collectors Club has an active branch in County Durham. Group digs by club members have produced many excellent bottles, pipes and pot lids from dumps around the Tyne and Wear estuaries. The county has no canals; most dumps are sited in worked-out quarries and clay pits around the main towns, though village dumps in

the county have also been profitably explored. Near
Sunderland several sites have been found along the banks of
streams north of the town; at Chester-le-Street local quarries are rich in Victorian refuse; Teesside dumps in
abandoned quarries and clay pits at Hartlepool, Stockton

Fig. 46 A fine display
in a northern bottle
shop.

Fig. 47 Bottles from a dump in County Durham.

and Redcar have produced many dark green Codd's and a number of blue Hamilton's.

The most profitable coinshooting sites in the county are parks and open spaces around Durham City where many Victorian coins have been found on local moors and along the grassy banks of the River Wear. At Sunderland the tidal foreshores of this river have produced eighteenth- and nineteenth-century relics, and many Roman coins have been found on the Tyne foreshore between Gateshead and Jarrow. Good finds have also been made at Barnard Castle

beneath the bridge across the Tees where river raking produces medieval and later coins and relics. Similar results can be expected beneath the bridge at Yarm further downstream.

Fig. 48 Pot lids from dumps in County Durham.

In the eighteenth and nineteenth centuries cock-fighting, bare-knuckle boxing, and greyhound coursing with live hares were popular sports in County Durham. The main centre for these activities was Bishop Auckland where large crowds from all parts of the county gathered on the Hunwick, Byers Green, and Etherley moors to gamble fortunes on the bloody outcome of each event. In April 1751 a Captain Milbank and a Doctor Dunn fought a sixteen round cock-fight which cost the lives of thirty-one cocks. Stakes were ten guineas each battle with 200 guineas for the ultimate winner. Captain Milbank won by nine rounds to seven. Thousands of similar contests took place on the moors around the town where the vast crowds lost numerous coins

Fig. 49 Most of these amateur treasures were found on northern riversides.

and other relics which can be found today by efficient detector users.

Buried treasures discovered in the county include a hoard of seventh-century coins found near Heworth Chapel, Gateshead, in 1822; a large hoard of coins found in a field near the Roman fort at Piercebridge in 1921, and a small hoard of sixteenth-century silver pennies found in a field at West Hartburn in 1963. An exceptionally fine Elizabeth I shilling was dug up in the front garden of a house at Westgate-in-Weardale occupied by Mr George Bell in 1921. It is possible the coin came from a deeply buried hoard.

Northumberland has more Roman military remains and ruined medieval castles than any other county in Britain. Every river crossing, strategic hilltop and safe harbour has a brooding stronghold to remind visitors of the border strife which blighted the land for some fifteen hundred years as Romans, Picts, Saxons, Danes, Normans, Scots and English crossed and recrossed the wild moors in a never-ending round of invasion, retreat, conquest and defeat that has left a rich legacy of hoards, single coins and weapons of war beneath Northumbrian soil. The following gazetteer of sites where hoards and other relics have been found should guide any readers who take treasure-hunting holidays in this romantic county to exciting finds:

Northumberland

Alnmouth: An ancient port where the foreshores of the River Aln have recently produced medieval coins.

Amble: Roman coins have been found on Gloster Hill. Numerous wrecks have occurred around Coquet Island where Roman, Northumbrian and Scottish coins have been found. The island was once the centre for forgery and smuggling on this coast.

Bamburgh: Many coins and relics have been found in Budle Bay beneath the castle walls.

Beadnell: Drifting sand has covered part of the ancient harbour here.

Belford: Caves on Belford Moor are said to contain treasure; medieval finds have been made in them.

Berwick: The town changed hands thirteen times during wars between England and Scotland. Numerous relics of war have been found on the foreshores of the Tweed and on Halidon Hill where several battles took place. The best coinshooting sites are beneath the road bridge and further downstream at Tweedmouth.

Blyth: Eighteenth- and nineteenth-century coins can be found in the harbour.

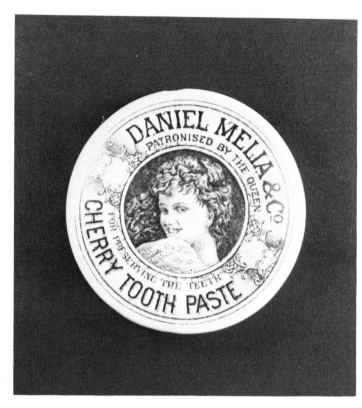

Capheaton: A rich hoard of Roman silver coins and plate was discovered in the eighteenth century in a field adjoining Silver Lane.

Carrawburgh: A total of 13,487 coins was found in a sacred well here in the nineteenth century.

Chesterholme: Local fields are rich in Roman coins. Many have also been found in the Bradley Burn, a local stream. A hoard of Roman gold and silver coins were found in a quarry on Thorngrafton Common in the nineteenth century.

Chollerford: Roman coins have been found beneath the site of the Roman bridge which crossed the North Tyne here.

Corbridge: Many finds of Roman and later coinage have

102

Fig. 51 Stoneware from Northumberland dumps.

been made on the banks of the Tyne here. Workmen found a pot of gold coins in a local field in 1911.

Craster: Roman and medieval coins have been found on the local foreshores near the ruins of Dunstanburgh Castle. The ancient harbour, now much silted, holds numerous relics.

Gosforth: Victorian coins have been found in High Gosforth Park.

Greatchesters: Many Roman coins have been dug up in the area.

Halton: Gold jewellery was found in Brunt Halfpenny Field here in 1802.

Housesteads: Many Roman coins have been found in local fields.

Howick: A Roman coin hoard was found in the eighteenth century in a field above Howick Burn.

Killingworth: A hoard of Roman gold and silver objects was found in 1811 at Backworth.

Fig. 52 A beautiful
bottle from
Northumberland.

Longframlington: A hoard of 300 gold nobles of
Edward III, Richard II and Henry IV were dug up
fifty yards south-west of the church in 1834.

Lucker: A Roman hoard was found in the nineteenth
century in a local peat bog.

Morpeth: Cannonballs were found several years ago below Castle Hill; medieval silver brooches were dug up in a field at Newminster in 1926.

Newburn: Many finds have been made in the river near the old ford across the Tyne.

Newcastle-on-Tyne: The foreshores of the river are rich in Roman, medieval and later relics. Many Victorian coins have been found on Town Moor and in Jesmond Dene.

Rudchester: A pot containing 500 Roman silver and 16 gold coins was dug up in 1766 near Rudchester Burn.

Throckley: In 1879 a hoard of 5,000 Roman coins was found in a field behind Hadrian's Wall here.

Tynemouth: Finds of all periods have been made on local foreshores.

Fig. 53 River Tees at Barnard Castle. A first-class coin and relic-hunting site.

Whittonstall: 1,200 silver coins of Edward I and Edward II were found here in 1958 by a labourer working on a site being prepared for a new police station.

Rockhounds are also well catered for in Northumberland. There are disused lead mines and unworked veins in the Cheviots where excellent quartz crystals can be found. Around Carshope in the Upper Coquet Valley specimens of amethyst have been located. Malachite and fluorite can also be found here and at Allenhead Town where there are many old mines. Agates and cornelians can be picked up along the banks of many streams in the Cheviot Hills and along the coast between Berwick and Tynemouth.

Bottle collecting in Northumberland is centred on the Tyne where riverside dumps downstream from Newcastle have produced many good finds.

Lake District rockhounding sites

There are three major gem-hunting areas in the Lake District and a visit to any one of them offers rockhounds opportunities to find a wide variety of specimens on the spoil heaps of abandoned mines.

Caldbeck Fells area: Lead, copper, silver, barytes, tungsten and china clay were formerly mined here. The most productive spoil heaps are found along the banks of Dale Beck south-west of Caldbeck village where malachite, blue and purple fluorite, rock crystal and calcite are found; and on the slopes of Carrock Fell where quartz, citrine, tourmaline, apatite and fluorite are obtainable.

Helvellyn area: Lead and haematite have been mined here. Most of the abandoned mines are to be found between Helvellyn and Ullswater where fluorite, quartz, pink barytes, cairngorm and tourmaline can be dug from spoil heaps.

Coniston area: Copper has been mined in this area, mainly around Birk Fell. Malachite, pyrites and rock crystal can be found on spoil heaps and in unworked veins.

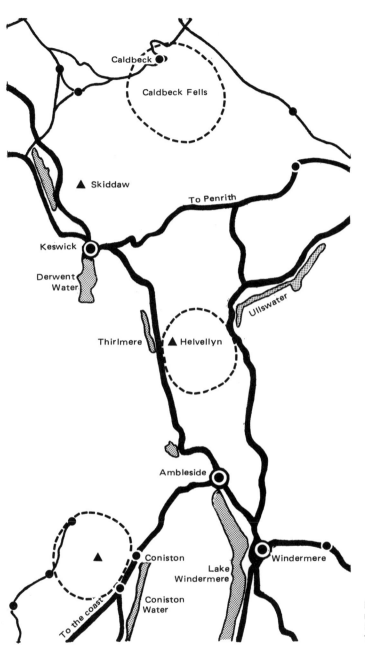

Fig. 54 Lake District
rockhounding sites.
Best locations are
within dotted lines.

Fig. 55

Fig. 56

Fig. 57

Lead has been mined in the Peak District of Derbyshire since Roman times and there are hundreds of abandoned mines with spoil heaps galore for hopeful rockhounds to explore. There are two main collecting areas:

Peak District rockhounding sites

Castleton–Eyam: This area is noted for bluejohn, the massive banded variety of fluorite. It is usually purple, though yellow specimens are occasionally found. Purple, red and yellow fluorite crystals can also be dug from spoil heaps in the area.

Matlock–Wirksworth: Spoil heaps in this area contain fluorite, malachite, haematite, smoky quartz and agate.

Fig. 58

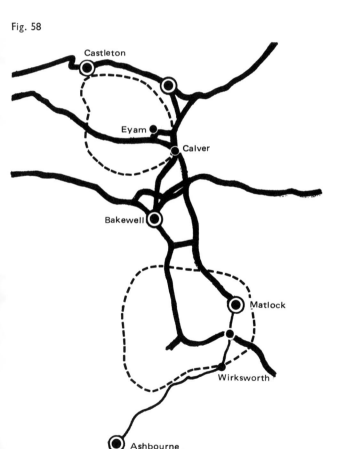

Fig. 55 Scene near an old mine in the Peak District.

Fig. 56 Winding gear at an old lead mine in the Derbyshire Peak District.

Fig. 57 Derbyshire Peak District, an excellent rockhounding area.

Fig. 58 Peak District rockhounding sites. The best locations are within dotted lines.

6 The East Coast

The southern foreshore of the Humber estuary from the mouth of the River Trent to South Ferriby has yielded numerous Roman coins to amateur treasure hunters. The Roman ferry across the Humber was at Winteringham and many of the best finds have been made there on a site one mile east of the modern village. At South Ferriby Roman and medieval coins have been found on the foreshore opposite Read's Island, and at Barton-on-Humber they have turned up in local fields. Downriver at Grimsby most of the finds made on the foreshore towards Cleethorpes have been modern, but earlier coins and relics have turned up on the banks of the River Freshney which flows into Grimsby docks. On the sea coast between Mablethorpe and Skegness Roman coins are regularly picked up on local beaches where, because of erosion, Roman and medieval settlements now lie between high and low tide marks. At Sutton-on-Sea the sandy beach has on several occasions been swept away by strong tides and remains of ancient buildings have been seen in the clay beneath. Skegness beach is rich in modern coins and jewellery.

Boston on the River Witham was once Lincolnshire's chief port. The tidal foreshores of the river hold many relics of the town's long history; they can be recovered by raking and sieving and by detector searches on gravel patches at the mouth of the river. It was somewhere in this region that King John lost his royal baggage in 1216 when crossing the Wash by a causeway suddenly overcome by the rising tide. Losses included two sets of coronation regalia together with jewels and silver bullion now worth millions of pounds and there is hardly a village within twenty miles of Boston that does not claim to hold the treasure within its parish boundaries. In recent years numerous attempts to recover the fortune have been made with equipment including detectors, divining rods, and even bulldozers, but so far nothing has been found. A very large hoard of silver coins dug up in 1932 during road-widening operations at Partney some twenty miles from Boston was at first claimed

Fig. 59 A bear's grease pot lid from Lincoln-shire.

by locals to be part of King John's treasure, but this was quickly proved incorrect when the hoard was examined by numismatists and found to consist largely of sixteenth-century coins. Most of the early coins found around the Wash south of Boston are Roman.

Many inland sites in the county have proved rich in treasure. In 1850 two Celtic gold torcs were found at Ulceby during the construction of a local railway, and in 1960 a hoard of 10,000 Roman coins was ploughed up a few miles away at Kirmington in a field west of the village. Single Roman coins have also turned up in other fields near Kirmington and at nearby Croxton where a hoard was found in the eighteenth century. West of Kirmington the villages of Broughton and Hibaldstow have yielded large numbers of Roman coins and relics including a valuable bronze statue ploughed up on Broughton Common in 1946.

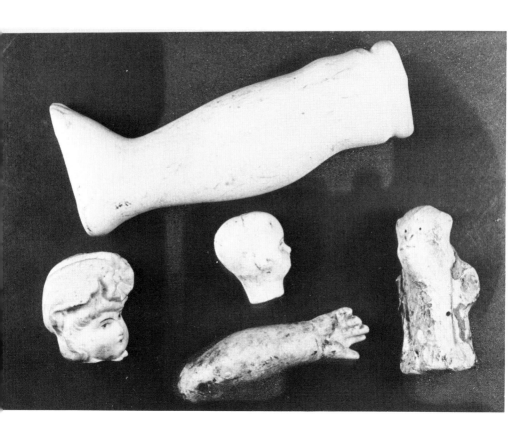

Many single coins of the Roman period have come to light
around the villages of Caistor and Claxby in mid-Lincoln-
shire, but the largest number of finds have undoubtedly
been made in and around Lincoln where there is hardly a
ploughed field that has not produced at least one Roman
coin. At Nettleham a hoard of bronze weapons was found
in the nineteenth century; at Stainfield a hoard was found
many years ago near Blackfield Close; and at Bardney large
numbers of coins have been found at Abbey Farm. A most
unusual find was made in 1928 in a field at Potter Hanworth
near Lincoln when a farmer ploughed up 18 Spanish gold
coins. They were one-hundred peseta pieces and had all been
minted during this century. No satisfactory explanation for
their sudden appearance in a Lincolnshire field was ever put
forward. More recently, in 1962, another farmer ploughed

112

up 700 silver coins of Elizabeth I, James I and Charles I on a farm at Stainton-by-Longworth a few miles from Lincoln. In the city a valuable hoard came to light in 1972 when a bricklayer dug up 20 silver discs while working on a school building site. He thought they were children's counters and forgot all about them until he saw similar discs in the city museum several days later and realized he had found Henry I pennies. More digging on the same spot produced a total of 750 coins.

Further south hundreds of finds have been made around Ancaster where a pot containing 2,000 Roman coins was ploughed up several years ago. A similar hoard was dug up a few miles away at Honington in the nineteenth century. At Sleaford numerous Celtic and Roman coins have been recovered from gardens and on allotment sites. When a new

Fig. 61 Finds from Lincolnshire rivers.

housing estate was built on Boston Road several years ago hundreds of coins and coin moulds were dug up. Saxon weapons and jewellery were also found in the nineteenth century during construction of the local railway line.

In addition to the tidal foreshore of the Humber there are two other riversides in Lincolnshire where exciting finds can be made by amateur treasure hunters. The River Trent from its mouth to Gainsborough is rich in productive sites. At Gainsborough, eighteenth-century coins have recently been found on the foreshore by amateur treasure hunters using detectors. At Owston Ferry further downstream a Roman hoard was discovered on the riverbank in 1953. Other coins including seventeenth-, eighteenth- and nineteenth-century specimens have also been found. At Barton-on-Stather the ancient ferry site across the Trent has also proved rich in seventeenth- and eighteenth-century coins and relics. The River Witham which flows into the Wash has yielded a variety of relics including the famous Witham Shield, a Celtic treasure found in 1826 when a bend in the river a few miles east of Lincoln was dredged. Further downstream at Tattershall Ferry a Celtic bronze trumpet was recovered from the riverbed in 1768. Since then many Roman and later coins have been found.

Bottle collectors in Lincolnshire have made many finds on the Humber estuary where Victorian refuse from Grimsby and from Hull in Yorkshire was dumped as part of land reclamation schemes. A stretch of overgrown canal near Caistor also contains Victorian refuse from these towns. The Louth Canal was used by barges transporting refuse to marshy areas along its banks, as was the now derelict Horncastle Canal which received much of Lincoln's late Victorian rubbish. British Bottle Collectors Club members have also held group digs in the county on sites at Scunthorpe and Sleaford. Many clay tobacco pipes and some bottles have come from the mouth of the River Witham.

Norfolk   Norfolk's beaches include some the the best pebble-hunting locations in Britain and holiday visitors to Cromer and Caistor rarely return home without a bucketful of attractive finds including agate, jasper, cornelian, and water-worn jet which is carried down the coast from Yorkshire by longshore drift. This coast is also the most likely place to find pieces of amber, some of which can be extremely valuable. Several years ago a man walking the foreshore near Cromer picked up a large piece which was later sold for £3,000. Even small pieces less than an inch in diameter can fetch several pounds if they contain the fossilized remains of insects; many such pieces have been found on Norfolk's coast in the past. The best time to hunt for amber is immediately following rough seas as the tide begins to fall. Being very light in weight the amber is cast onto the high tide line by breaking waves. Walk along one of these tidelines on any beach between Cromer and Caistor after stormy weather and you have a very good chance of finding large specimens.

It is worth taking a detector on one of these amber-hunting expeditions because many Victorian coins wash up on some of these beaches. At Cromer numerous finds have been made by holiday treasure hunters who have also found Roman coins on the beach and in local woods at nearby Sheringham. The beach and the old harbour at Wells are worth searching for eighteenth- and nineteenth-century coins, as is the coastline around Holme where medieval buildings are said to lie beneath the sand. At King's Lynn the harbour and the muddy riverside are rich in coins and relics of all periods from medieval to modern and excellent finds have been made in recent months by members of the British Amateur Treasure Hunting Club. The tidal fore-shores of the River Ouse upstream from King's Lynn are likely to prove equally rewarding for those equipped to search muddy locations.

Another river where excellent finds have been made is the Yare between Great Yarmouth and Norwich. Raking near Reedham and at Norwich has produced seventeenth- and eighteenth-century relics. Detector searches around Yarmouth have been rewarded with substantial amounts of Victorian coinage; modern coins have turned up in large numbers on beaches north and south of the town.

Fig. 62 (*above left*) A fine sealed bottle from a Norfolk dump.

Fig. 63 (*above right*) A Warner's 'Safe' Cure from Norfolk.

There can be few experienced bottle collectors who have not seen or heard of the beautiful dark green Codd's found on the vast refuse site between Norwich and Great Yarmouth where the Norfolk branch of the British Bottle Collectors Club has held many group digs. Unfortunately this site has not produced any of the equally well-known bloater paste pot lids for which Great Yarmouth is famous and which turn up regularly in most dumps around London. Research suggests many of them await discovery in dumps yet to be excavated along the banks of the overgrown canal between North Walsham and Great Yarmouth. Undiscovered dumps along the banks of the River Ouse above King's Lynn might also hold some of these prizes; a number of late Victorian bottles have recently been found in the river near Downham Market.

One of Britain's richest buried treasures was found in Norfolk in December, 1948, at the tiny village of Snettisham a few miles from King's Lynn. At the beginning of December in that year a local ploughman working on Ken Hill turned up what he thought were three worthless pieces of iron. After inspecting the objects briefly he threw them on waste ground at the edge of the field where they remained for several days until more oddly shaped metal objects and a number of coins were revealed by the plough. Close inspection showed the metal to be pure gold and a hurried search was made for the 'worthless pieces of iron' discarded at the edge of the field a few days earlier. When cleaned they proved to be Celtic gold torcs, the largest of which measured nine inches in diameter.

At this point a local archaeologist was called in and it was as he was inspecting the area around the hole from which the second hoard had come that a third discovery was made—a hoard of extremely rare Celtic coins dated 87–85 BC. The treasures found were undoubtedly the richest ever to come from Norfolk soil; but the final total had yet to be reached. In the last week of December the ploughman uncovered a fourth hoard of gold and tin coins in the same field, proving once again that treasure is most likely to be found in those places where it has already been found.

Several other Celtic gold torcs have been found in Norfolk fields. Sites include Ashill, Bittering Common and Terrington St Clements where a torc found in 1941 was thrown away by a ploughman who thought it was an old door knocker. Fortunately it was taken to a local museum by another man and indentified as Celtic gold. Other hoards from Norfolk soil include 200 gold nobles of Edward III found by workmen digging a drain at Fakenham, and 800 Saxon coins found in 1958 in the grounds of Wymondham College by workmen digging the foundations of a house. In 1962 a farmer at Hockwold found a rich hoard of Roman silverware in a local wood.

Suffolk   It was in Suffolk during the winter of 1940 that the richest buried treasure ever found in Britain was unearthed. The story of its finding and the Treasure Trove inquest which followed make interesting reading and provide valuable lessons for present-day treasure hunters. It began in February 1940, when tractor driver Gordon Butcher ploughed a four-acre plot on Thistly Green, a large common field on the outskirts of Mildenhall. Many single Roman coins had been found in the field prior to 1940 and most of them had come into the possession of a man named Arthur Ford who had hired Butcher for this particular job. The plot Butcher had been instructed to plough was to be planted with sugarbeet later in the year and Ford told Butcher to plough deeply, as is required for sugarbeet, and also to keep his eyes open for any coins the plough might unearth.

Later that day Butcher's ploughshare struck a buried object and the wooden pin connecting the tractor to the plough was broken by the impact. When he stepped down to investigate the cause of the trouble Butcher unearthed with his bare hands a large metal dish measuring more than two feet in diameter. Realizing it must be of a great age Butcher went to fetch Arthur Ford and while Ford looked on the tractor driver dug out another thirty-two dishes, spoons, and other metal objects hidden beneath the larger dish. Ford told Butcher the metal was pewter and that he would like to have the finds for his collection. Butcher did not share his employer's interest in old things and did not object when Ford placed all the objects in a potato sack and took them home.

There matters rested for six years until an archaeologist who occasionally bought unwanted coins from Arthur Ford visited Ford's home and saw on his sideboard a shining silver dish richly decorated with mythological scenes. Recognizing it at once as an object of great value he pressed Ford to show him the other finds which the farmer had not yet cleaned. One glance at them convinced the archaeologist the entire hoard was extremely valuable and he insisted Ford should report the find immediately to the British Museum.

At the Treasure Trove inquest held a few weeks later museum officials stated the hoard was a third-century Romano-British silver treasure and they estimated its value at more than £1,000,000. Ford insisted he had not realized the metal was silver; Butcher said simply that he had handed the finds to his employer and never thought about the incident since. The coroner had no hesitation in declaring the find to be Treasure Trove; he also declared that neither Ford nor Butcher would receive the full market value of the hoard because the find had been concealed for six years. Instead they received £1,000 each in token payment for a treasure that is now one of the prized possessions of the British Museum and probably worth several times the estimate made of its value in 1946.

Few people disagree that Gordon Butcher, the finder of the Mildenhall Treasure, was a most unlucky man. When he handed the finds to his boss he did what any honest working man would have done; but he did break the Treasure Trove laws, and ignorance of those laws together with the inability to distinguish silver from pewter cost him £999,000. Moral: Abide by the Treasure Trove laws and make quite sure you can recognize gold and silver when you see them encrusted with dirt and oxidization.

A less valuable but equally exciting find was made in Ipswich in 1968 when a bulldozer driver working on a building site in Halcolme Crescent dug up five Celtic gold torcs during earthmoving operations. He reported the finds immediately and subsequently received a Treasure Trove reward of £45,000. In 1970 when the houses in Halcolme Crescent were sold one resident dug his new garden and turned up another gold torc on the end of his fork. A similar find was made in a garden at Boyton in the nineteenth century.

Single Celtic and Roman coins have turned up in ploughed fields near several villages and towns in Suffolk—Saxmundham, Stowmarket, Bury St Edmunds, Sudbury, Debenham and Glemsford. In 1926 a hoard was found near a chalk pit at Coddenham where dozens of coins had been picked up over many years, and in 1969 a field at Laken-

Fig. 64 Mineral water bottles from Suffolk sites.

heath known locally as Roman Field yielded a pot containing 500 gold, silver and bronze coins.

On the coast there are excellent coinshooting sites near Lowestoft where many Victorian coins have been found in the harbour, and at Southwold where medieval coins and relics have recently been discovered on the beach. There is a fascinating stretch of coastline around Aldburgh which never fails to produce good finds. The ancient port of Dunwich has been partly lost to the sea here and many relics have been found on the beach. In 1911 particularly high tides on this coast removed large quantities of sand from the beach at nearby Thorpe Ness to reveal thousands of coins, rings, ornaments, tokens, badges, and numerous other finds which kept local beachcombers very busy for several weeks. There are still large amounts of unrecovered valuables on this stretch of coast. Further south the muddy foreshores of the Rivers Orwell and Deben hold many prizes. Roman, Saxon, Elizabethan and Victorian finds have recently been made by amateur treasure hunters.

It is around these two rivers that most Suffolk bottle-collecting activities take place. The Deben estuary was used by London's refuse barges in the late nineteenth century and there are dumps along its banks between Bawdsey and Woodbridge. Most of the dumps found on low-lying land around the mouth of the Orwell contain Victorian refuse from Ipswich. The riverbanks are exceptionally rich in clay tobacco pipes. Elsewhere in Suffolk dumps have been dug by the British Bottle Collectors Club along the banks of the River Waveney near Lowestoft and along the canal near Stowmarket.

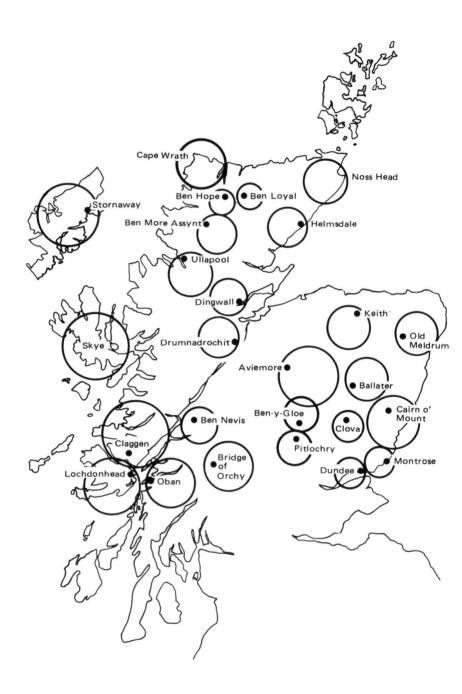

Cape Wrath

Noss Head

Stornaway

Ben Hope ● ● Ben Loyal

Ben More Assynt ● ● Helmsdale

Ullapool ●

Dingwall ●

Skye

Drumnadrochit ●

Keith ●

Old Meldrum ●

Aviemore ●

Ballater ●

Ben-y-Gloe

Cairn o' Mount ●

Ben Nevis ●

Clova

Claggen

Pitlochry ●

Bridge of Orchy

Montrose ●

Lochdonhead ●

● Oban

Dundee

7 Scotland

Bottle collecting and coinshooting are relatively unknown hobbies in Scotland, at present pursued by only a handful of pioneers concentrated around Edinburgh and Glasgow. For this reason little is yet known about sites in other areas, but if they prove even half as productive as those already tested around the major cities the future of the hobbies in Scotland is assured.

Favoured sites for the disposal of household refuse around both cities appear to have been clay pits near brickworks and low-lying land on the banks of the Forth and Clyde. On the Forth, dumps between Granton and Grangemouth have already produced a number of attractive stoneware whisky flasks and some beautiful pot lids; on the Clyde a large number of clay tobacco pipes and many Hamilton's which appear to have been used as ships' ballast have come to light. Richly embossed whisky bottles have also been dug up in large numbers.

Edinburgh and Glasgow

Fig. 65 *(facing)* Rock-hounding sites in the Scottish Highlands.

Fig. 66 Bottles from a Glasgow dump.

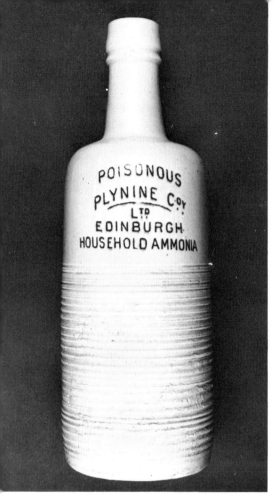

POISONOUS
PLYNINE Cᵒʸ
Lᵀᴰ
EDINBURGH
HOUSEHOLD AMMONIA

CRUISKEEN LAWN

MITCHELL'S

OLD
IRISH WHISKY

BELFAST

Fig. 67 (*above left*) From an Edinburgh rubbish dump.

Fig. 68 (*above right*) From a dump near Glasgow.

It is on the foreshores of these two great rivers that most Scottish detector owners have tried their luck in recent years. The harbour and beach at Leith have yielded seventeenth- and eighteenth-century coins and the area around the mouth of the River Almond has proved rich in Roman coins. In 1922 a hoard of 244 Roman coins was ploughed up in a field near this river on the outskirts of Linlithgow. A similar find was made nearby in the nineteenth century. Parks and open spaces in both Edinburgh and Glasgow hold substantial amounts of Victorian coinage and jewellery and an initial survey of the southern foreshore of the Clyde indicates that many exciting finds from medieval to modern

await discovery between Broomielaw and Greenock. Two or three valuable medieval coins have been recovered on the foreshore beneath Dumbarton Castle.

On the Ayrshire coast popular beaches have so far yielded only modern finds but the area is rich in ruined castles and ancient ports and it seems likely that earlier coins and relics will be found when the number of detector owners increases. In 1924 workmen demolishing an old cottage in High Street, Ayr, found a pot containing 638 coins of Mary, Queen of Scots. Dumfriesshire has produced exciting finds

The South

Fig. 70 Stoneware from a Scottish dump.

in the past. An exceptionally fine coin of Edward I was found at Newton Farm, Thornhill, in 1937; its condition indicates the possibility of an undiscovered hoard here. Many Roman coins and several Celtic gold specimens have also been found near Birrenswark and on the riverside near Dumfries, while hills around Castle Douglas hold Roman and medieval specimens. Berwickshire has also proved rich in hoards; they have been ploughed up on Lamberton Moor, at Carlingwark, and at Blackburn Mill where finds included gold coins. On the east coast Civil War coins have been found on the beach near Tantallon Castle at North Berwick, and sixteenth-century coins have come from the harbour at Dunbar. In Lanarkshire numerous finds of Celtic, Roman and medieval coins and relics have been made on Louden Hill near the Ayrshire border and on the banks of the River Mouse near Lanark. A hoard of silver and gold coins was found several years ago at Lesmahgow.

The lure of gold has for centuries drawn men to the hills

of Lanarkshire where river and stream gravels were once the richest source of gold in Britain. In the fifteenth and sixteenth centuries productive veins were found in the Wanlockhead area and gold mining became an important industry employing several hundred men for many years. By the nineteenth century these accessible veins were almost exhausted and Britain had found new and unexploited sources in Australia, Canada and other parts of her empire; Scottish gold became too expensive to mine and commercial operations ceased. Nevertheless the hardy folks who live in these hills continued to obtain gold until quite recently. Most of the older women in the district have wedding rings made of gold from local streams and now that the price of the metal has soared to undreamed of heights a few old men who still possess the skills have turned once more to their gold pans. For those who wish to join them the essential tools are a gold pan, a strong shovel, and lots of patience. A riffle board or a suction dredge greatly improve chances of success and are recommended to those contemplating serious gold-hunting expeditions. Instruc-

Fig. 71 (*above left*) Gold-bearing stream in Lanarkshire.

Fig. 72 (*above right*) Riffle board for gold hunting in Scotland.

127

Fig. 73 (*above*) Crofts in Ross and Cromarty where small 19th-century bottle dumps should be easy to find.

Fig. 74 (*right*) Mountain streams in Scotland hold many semi-precious gems.

tions on using the equipment are given in my earlier book, *Treasure Hunting for All*.

In the past the most productive gold-bearing gravels were found on the bed of the River Elvan between Wanlockhead and Elvanfoot. Nowadays it is the narrow streams feeding the main watercourse which must be searched in the hope of finding alluvial deposits. Streams flowing northwards towards the River Duneaton are also known to be gold-bearing, as are streams in the hills above Sanquhar. The best time of the year to visit the region is in summer when the level of water in these streams has fallen to expose gravel on their beds. Deep digging is essential in order to reach the bedrock on which large particles of gold are always found.

A visit to this part of Scotland is worthwhile even if the gold in the hills proves elusive. There are numerous old

lead mines where specimens of fluorite, malachite, azurite and rock crystal can be obtained. Many of the spoil heaps can be seen from the road which runs from Ledhills to Mennock; others—less frequently visited—lie high in the hills between Mennock Pass and Dalveen Pass. To the south-west amethyst is found in quarries and unworked veins around New Abbey. Excellent specimens of malachite, rock crystal, jasper and agate can be obtained in the hills around Castle Douglas and New Galloway which is also noted for its tourmaline. The coasts in this region have excellent pebble beaches where all of the above specimens can be found.

In the east the Moorfoot Hills between Peebles and Carlops can be profitably explored for agate which is found in many quarries and in unworked veins. Good finds including chalcedony have been made around rocky outcrops in Teviotdale and Lauderdale and along the coast from Berwick to Dunbar where attractive agate pebbles are found in large numbers. Similar finds can be made on holiday beaches in the Firth of Forth and near St Andrews in Fifeshire. In the hills of Renfrewshire and in the Campsie Fells north of Glasgow quarries and stream banks are rich in agate and rock crystal; specimens of cairngorm are also occasionally found.

The North Northern Scotland is Britain's last wilderness, much of it still awaiting a detailed geological survey and with hundreds of square miles intimately known to only a handful of shepherds and gamekeepers. It is also a region rich in volcanic rocks which make it a rockhound's paradise where anything from a humble agate pebble to a valuable diamond or even a sapphire might be found. Because of their remoteness many of the best gem-hunting areas are visited during less than three months each year and then only by a tiny fraction of Britain's rockhounding enthusiasts who invariably return from their lonely expeditions overloaded with exciting finds. Readers with sufficient stamina for the trip and a determination to own a display cabinet of superb specimens are urged to join them. Adventurous bottle

collectors and treasure hunters prepared for long and lonely searches around derelict castles and abandoned crofts where the only certainty is that no one has searched before should also make the journey.

Sapphires are said to have been found on Mull and in neighbouring Argyllshire but locations were never disclosed. They might have come from the mountains around Lochdonhead where excellent specimens of tourmaline and epidote can be found, or east of Oban where there are many unexplored veins containing cairngorm. North of Mull the mainland rocks around Claggen contain garnet, flourite, kyonite, epidote, tourmaline, and much agate. Visitors to Ben Nevis should find sphene, and the Moor of Rannock in the Grampians north of Bridge of Orchy is rich in cairngorm, topaz and beryl.

131

The Cairngorm Mountains south of Aviemore are the most productive source of the gem that bears their name; a single cavity once yielded ten hundredweights to a lucky prospector. Beryl and topaz can also be found. Recently a young girl on holiday here picked up a huge crystal on a footpath. To the south around Ben-y-Gloe there are rich deposits of serpentine and fluorite, while the area around Pitlochry is noted for garnets.

East coast beaches in Angus, Kincardine and Aberdeen-shire hold numerous agates which can also be found at inland sites with amethyst and cairngorm in Angus. The area around Cairn o' Mount in Kincardineshire has produced large specimens of tourmaline and epidote, and the Dee valley around Ballater has beryl and fluorite. Quarries near Old Meldrum in Aberdeenshire can be profitably explored for tourmaline, while the area around Keith in Banffshire is rich in citrine, cairngorm and rock crystal. On the western shores of Loch Ness in the Drumnadrochit region there are numerous veins and deposits of serpentine, zircon, garnet, cairngorm and beryl. The Isle of Skye is also rich in serpentine and many finds of agate, beryl and cairngorm have been made by holiday visitors. Lewis is less well-known to tourists but it is a favourite rockhounding island where cairngorm, beryl, topaz, garnet, zircon and olivine can all be found. Ullapool in Ross and Cromarty is another excellent district for cairngorm, agate, garnet and beryl.

In the far north the moors and mountains of Caithness and Sutherland are even less frequently visited than gem-hunting locations further south. Tiny diamonds are often found around Ben Hope where a few large specimens have also been discovered in the past. Even without its diamonds the area is worth visiting for its rich sources of fluorite, cairn-gorm, tourmaline and zircon. Garnets can be found around Cape Wrath, Ben Loyal, and Ben More Assynt where they are accompanied by olivine, serpentine, fluorite, beryl, spinel and tourmaline. In Caithness the area west of Noss Head is noted for fluorite, rock crystal, cairngorm and spinel.

Lastly there is Sutherland's gold which would make

132

Northern Scotland worth visiting even if there were no gemstones to be found. No one knows how much gold there is in the county, but its value is counted in tens of thousands of pounds by the most conservative geologists and in hundreds of thousands of pounds by optimistic prospectors who have seen it sparkling in their gold pans. Unlike the Lanarkshire deposits Sutherland's gold was not exploited before the nineteenth century when a nugget weighing one and a half ounces was found in Kildonan Burn in 1840. A handful of local people in the Helmsdale area then began to supplement their incomes from sheep and fishing by panning the local streams, but it was not until 1868 when an experienced gold miner named Gilchrist, who had spent many years in Australia, visited the region that commercial exploitation began. Gilchrist and a handful of his goldmining friends

Fig. 76 Most beaches in Scotland are rich in agate pebbles.

Fig. 77 Rockhounding
country on the Isle of
Skye.

extracted large amounts of gold during that year from the Suisgill Burn and soon the news of their strike attracted hundreds of adventurers, tinkers and down-and-outs to Helmsdale where for a few months they found employment at the 'diggings' and helped to recover gold valued then at £50,000. Much of the metal came from easily worked gravels on the edges of the Suisgill and Kinbrace Burns where even inexperienced panners could recover it in payable quantities. These easy pickings were exhausted within a year when most of the men drifted away and Britain's last 'gold rush' came to an end.

Only Gilchrist and the few men he took with him to Sutherland had experience of gold recovery and they alone constructed sluices, dams and tail races. Most of the other hopefuls relied on frying pans and tin plates because there was nowhere they could buy gold pans. As they were getting only a few shillings an ounce for the gold they recovered it is not difficult to understand why they became disheartened long before the entire wealth of those mountain streams was exhausted. Indeed, it seems likely they extracted only a tiny fraction of Sutherland's gold; geologists are now convinced that untouched deposits lie on the moors on both sides of Helmsdale. Present-day treasure hunters have proved beyond doubt that streams for twenty miles inland from Helmsdale hold alluvial gold in sufficient quantities to make recovery worthwhile. With sound equipment including small-loop detectors for locating nuggets and lots of determination to carry on the search when the going gets tough most readers should find their share. Good hunting!

Fig. 78 The wilds of Sutherland.

The amateur treasure hunters' Code of Conduct

1. Don't interfere with archaeological sites or ancient monuments. Join your local archaeological society if you are interested in ancient history.

2. Don't leave a mess. It is perfectly simple to extract a coin or other small object buried a few inches under the ground without digging a great hole. Use a sharpened trowel or a knife to cut a neat circle; extract the object; replace the soil and grass carefully and even *you* will have difficulty in finding the spot again.

3. Help keep Britain tidy—and help yourself. Bottle tops, silver paper, and tin cans are the last things you should throw away. You could well be digging them up again next year. So do yourself and the community a favour by taking all rusty junk you find to the nearest litter bin.

4. Don't trespass. Ask permission before venturing onto any private land.

5. Report all unusual historical finds to your local museum and get expert help if you accidentally discover a site of archaeological interest.

6. Learn the Treasure Trove laws and report all finds of gold and silver objects to the police. You will be well rewarded if the objects you find are declared Treasure Trove.

7. Respect the Country Code. Don't leave gates open when crossing fields and don't damage crops or frighten animals.

8. Never miss an opportunity to show and explain your detector to anyone who asks about it. Be friendly. You could pick up some clues to a good site.

9. If you meet another detector user while out on a hunt introduce yourself. You could probably teach each other a lot.

10. Finally, remember that when you are out with your detector you are an ambassador for the whole amateur treasure hunting fraternity. Don't give us a bad name.

Useful addresses and further reading

When writing to any of the addresses listed below to obtain leaflets, catalogues, or information you must enclose a stamped addressed envelope if you require a prompt reply.

Clubs

E.itish Bottle Collectors Club, The Secretary, 19 Hambro Avenue, Rayleigh, Essex.
British Amateur Treasure Hunters Club, The Secretary, Colet Road, Hutton, Brentwood, Essex.

Suppliers of equipment

Joan Allen Electronics Ltd
   184 Main Road, Biggin Hill, Kent.
Treasure Hunting Supplies
   71 Caledonian Road, London N.W.1.
M.L. Beach (Products) Ltd
   41 Church Street, Twickenham, Middlesex.
Collectors Old Bottle Room
   184 Main Road, Biggin Hill, Kent.
Old Bottle Cellar
   71 Caledonian Road, London N.W.1.
The Bottle Shop
   139 Wilton Street, Northwich, Cheshire.

Publications

Bottles and Relics News (monthly magazine), 'Greenacres', Church Road, Black Notley, Braintree, Essex.

Other books by the same author:
Pebble Polishing (Blandford Press)
Rock and Gem Polishing (Blandford Press)
Bottle Collecting (Blandford Press)
Treasure Hunting For All (Blandford Press)
Digging up Antiques (Pitman)
Collecting Pot Lids (Pitman)
Marble Bottles (Bottles and Relics Publications)

Ginger Beer Collector's Guide (Bottles and Relics Publications)
The Best of British Bottles (Bottles and Relics Publications)

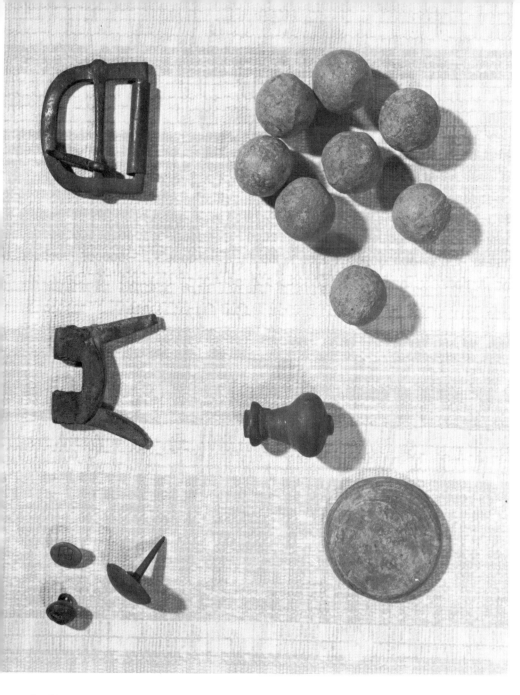

Fig. 79 Typical riverside foreshore finds, found on a low tide beneath
Blackfriars Bridge on the Thames.